With the compliments of

Mrs. George A. Plimpton

            The Lewis Farm
            Walpole, Massachusetts

SHAKESPEARE

The portrait bears a date, "aet: 46-1610". It is signed "Lynde" (unknown). Property of the author

THE EDUCATION
OF SHAKESPEARE

*Illustrated from the Schoolbooks
in Use in his Time*

BY

GEORGE A. PLIMPTON

LONDON & NEW YORK
OXFORD UNIVERSITY PRESS
1933

To My Wife

FANNY HASTINGS PLIMPTON

Preface

IT HAS been my privilege to get together the manuscripts and books which are more or less responsible for our present civilization, because they are the books from which the youth of many centuries have received their education. From this collection I have picked out the textbooks in use at the time that Shakespeare was in school. All the books from which I quote are on my own shelves. There are others, but I have confined this study to my own collection. I do not pretend to have made any study of the various controversies about Shakespeare, I do not profess to be a Shakespearean scholar; but I happen to own some books which are of interest to scholars, and I feel competent to give a simple and informal description of them. In the illustrations, however, it has not been possible to indicate the format of the original books. To those who want a more detailed study I recommend Foster Watson's *English Grammar Schools to 1660* (Cambridge University Press) and H. R. D. Anders's *Shakespeare's Books* (Berlin, 1904, Georg Reimer), to both of which I am much indebted, and from which I have quoted frequently. I am also indebted to George Lyman Kittredge, for reading the manuscript, to David Eugene Smith, and especially to Mrs. Plimpton, for her constant help.

Contents

THE EDUCATION
OF SHAKESPEARE

TITLE-PAGE OF THE MARGARITA PHILOSOPHICA

I. *Introduction*

SHAKESPEARE did not write an autobiography, and our knowledge of him is limited. We know that he was born in 1564. He probably went to the Stratford Grammar School, and was there presumably until 1580. This study purposes first to outline the education usual in those days, as described in the books written for teachers, showing what should be taught, and how it should be taught, and secondly to describe and quote from some of the textbooks in use during Shakespeare's schooldays.

Before taking up the detail of instruction at his time let us examine the sort of education that had come down from ancient days; this cannot be better illustrated than by the Margarita Philosophica, first printed in 1503.

The Margarita Philosophica, from which the picture of the Tower of Knowledge is taken, was the first modern encyclopedia of any note, based on the late Latin models. The author, Gregorius Reisch (born at Balingen, Württemberg; died at Freiburg, in 1523), studied at Freiburg (1487), where he received his bachelor's and master's degrees. He became a Carthusian, and was made prior at Freiburg, and confessor to Maximilian I; he was also the teacher of Eck and Waldseemüller, and assistant to Erasmus. The Margarita Philosophica consists of twelve books, and contains a compendium of the Trivium, the Quadrivium, and the natural and moral sciences. Its popularity is shown by its having been published in sixteen editions in the course of

3

TOWER OF KNOWLEDGE, SHOWING STAGES
IN MEDIEVAL EDUCATION

From the Margarita Philosophica, 1504

a century. The Tower of Knowledge (p. 4) represents the general scheme of education from old Roman days down to the time of Shakespeare and even beyond. To enter the Tower, the child learns his letters from a hornbook, and the door is unlocked with a key named Grammar. His first teacher is Donatus, of the fourth century, the teacher of St. Jerome. Donatus wrote an elementary Latin Grammar that was widely used for a thousand years. During the Middle Ages this book was known as the *Donat*.[1] The child goes next up a flight of stairs, and continues his study of Latin in the grammar by Priscian (flourished A.D. 500), "the last of the old Romans". His arithmetic is by Boethius (about 480–524), his rhetoric by Cicero, his logic by Aristotle, his astronomy by Ptolemy, his geometry by Euclid, and his music by Pythagoras.

Here we have the three language studies, grammar, logic, and rhetoric, and the four science studies, arithmetic, geometry, music, and astronomy, the first group (of three studies) being called the Trivium, and the second group the Quadrivium. To these were added moral philosophy by Seneca, and natural philosophy by Pliny; and the whole was capped in the Middle Ages by theology, here represented by Abelard's pupil Peter Lombard, who died in 1164.

[1] The first book Gutenberg printed (even before the Bible) was a Donatus (*c.* 1450) of which I have a single leaf.

Th. Eliott Knight.

ELYOT
Frontispiece of Elyot's *Castell of Helth*

II. *Teachers in Shakespeare's Day*

SIR THOMAS ELYOT

BEARING in mind the general scheme of education shown in the Tower of Knowledge, let us examine the theories of some of the educators in Shakespeare's day. One of the greatest of these writers was Sir Thomas Elyot, who was born about 1490, and died in 1546. Elyot was a gentleman, member of Parliament for Cambridge, ambassador, and scholar. His friendship with More and Erasmus may have injured his career. Among his books we are concerned with *The gouernour* (London, 1557), which embodies his ideas about teachers, especially the educators of princes.

This "boke named *The gouernour* deuised by sir Thomas Elyot Knyght" treats of education of "them" that may hereafter be deemed worthy to be "gouernours of the publike weale".

As soon as children can talk, "instil in them swete maners and vertuous custome. Provide companions irreproachable".

Here is an outline of Elyot's theories.

I. *Up to Age of Seven:*

    A. First letters — let them be painted in pleasant manner.

    B. Latin

        1. Teach the child to speak Latin.

           a. Teach names in Latin of objects in sight and parts of body.

7

      b. Give him something he especially desires if he will ask for it in Latin.

  2. Let the nobleman instruct or at least examine his own child in Latin (better than dice or cards).

  3. People about him must speak pure and elegant Latin, even his nurses, if possible. In any case, let no English be spoken except what is "clene, polite, perfectly, and articulately pronounced, omittynge no letter or sillable".

II. *From Seven to Fourteen Years:*

A. Take the child from the company of women (with the exception of one "aunciente and sadde matrone").

B. A Tutor

  1. "An aunciente and worshypful man"; if also learned, so much the better. (Character first; gentleness mixed with gravity.)

    (Kind of teachers wanted by School Authorities: "That neither the master nor vsher shall be common gamesters, haunters of tauerns; neither to exceed in apparel, nor any other ways to be an infamy to the school, or to giue euil example to the scholars, to whom in all points they ought to show themselves examples of honest, continent and godly behauior". — Oundle, 1556)

  2. Office of the tutor
    a. To know the nature of his pupil and hold up before him virtues, and to make him see the enormity of vice.
    b. To guard the child against overwork.

C. Music

  1. Valuable as a recreation.
    Examples: David, Achilles (his harp calms him), and Alexander.

  2. Beware of overdoing this.
    Example: Nero.

  3. A nobleman's son should not perform in public.

D. Painting and carving commendable.

E. Order of learning. Greek and Latin should be studied at one time, but it is permitted to begin with Greek (this being the harder). Begin at seven.

During three years study Greek authors. At the same time do not fail to speak Latin. Do not tire the child with Greek and Latin grammar. It is better to give a few quick rules of grammar interlaced with reading.

> Grammer, beyng but an introduction to the vnderstandyng of autours, if it be made to lōg or exquisite to the lerner it in a maner mortifieth his courage: And by that tyme he cometh to the moste swete and pleasant redynge of olde auctours, the sparkes of feruent desyre of lernyng is extinct, with the burdeyne of grāmer, like as a litle fire is sone quèched with a great heape of smal stickes: so that it can neuer come to the principal logges, wher it shulde long burne in a great pleasant fire.

F. Reading

    1. Æsop's Fables in Greek.
        a. Make the child understand the fable.
        b. Apply it to his conduct.
        c. Commit the lessons to memory.

    2. Lucian. Some quick and merry dialogues.

    3. Or Aristophanes.

    4. *Homer* — "Noble Homer".
        No lesson for a young gentleman is to be compared with Homer if he be plainly and substantially expounded and declared by the master.

    5. Virgil will furnish everything apt to the child's wit. He is to be preferred before any other Latin author.
        a. Æneid.
        b. Bucolics.
        c. Georgics.
        Let the child make verses in imitation of Virgil and Homer.

6. Ovid
   a. Metamorphoses.
   b. De Fastis.
      (Do not spend too much time on these.)
7. Horace.
8. Silius and Lucan.
9. Hesiod.
   Do not have the child read *all* these books, but have instruction enough in each to get *some profit* from them.

III. *From Fourteen to Seventeen Years:*
   (This period Shakespeare probably missed.)
   A. Logic
      "Topica" of Cicero or Agricola, one half year.

   B. Rhetoric (Hermogenes or Quintilian)
      1. Especially Persuasion.
      2. Copiam Verborum et Rerum of Erasmus.
      3. Isocrates.
      4. Demosthenes and Tulli.

   C. Cosmography
      1. To help in understanding history.
      2. Use Ptolemy's tables.

   D. History
      1. Livy.
      2. Xenophon
         Cyropædia
      3. Quintus Curtius.
         (Defer Julius Cæsar and Sallust till student has had some experience.)
      4. Tacitus.

IV. *Seventeen Years:*
   A. Philosophy, especially moral (read to him).
      1. Aristotle's Ethics (in Greek).
      2. Cicero's De Officiis.
      3. Plato.
      4. Proverbs of Solomon and Ecclesiastes.

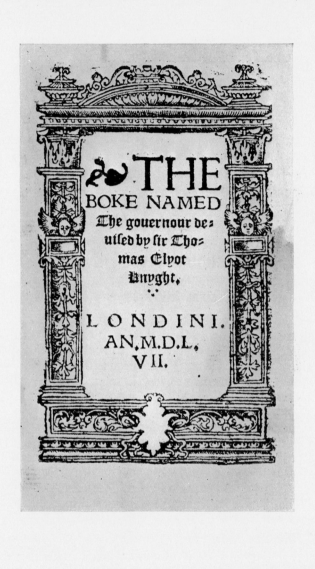

TITLE-PAGE OF ELYOT'S *BOKE NAMED THE GOVERNOVR*

B. Historical parts of the Bible.
C. Erasmus's Instruction of a Christian Prince.
D. Study of English laws (at 21 years).

V. *Physical Education from Fourteen Years Up:*

A. Walking.
B. Throwing stone or bar.
C. Tennis.
D. Wrestling.
E. Running.
F. Swimming.
G. Handling weapons.
H. Riding.
I. Hunting.
J. Dancing.
K. Shooting with a long bow.

Elyot now proceeds as follows:

The second occasion, wherefore gentyl mens children seldome haue sufficiēt lerning, is auarice. For where theyr
parentes wylle not aduenture, to sende thē farre oute of
theyr propre countreis, partly for feare of deathe, whiche
perchaunce dare not approche them at home with their
father, partlye for expence of money, whiche they suppose
woulde be lesse in their owne houses, or in a village with
some of their tenantes or frendes, hauing seldome any re-
garde to the teacher, whether he be wel learned or ignorant.
For if they hyre a schole maister to teache in their houses,
they chiefely enquere, with how smal a salary he wyl be
contented, and neuer doo inserch how much good lernyng
he hath, and how amonge wel learned men, he is therein
esteemed: vsynge therin lesse diligence than in takyng
seruantes, whose seruice is of muche lesse importance, and
to a good scholemaister, is not in profite to be compared.

A gentilman, er he take a cooke in his seruice, wyl fyrste
examyne hym diligently, how many sortes of meates,
potages, and sauces he can perfectly make, and howe wel
he can season them: that they may be bothe plesaunt and
nouryshynge. yea, and if it be but a fauconer, he wyll

scrupulouslye enquire, what skyl he hath in feedynge, called diete, and kepyng of his hauke from al syknes: Also howe he can reclaime her, and prepare her to flighte. And to suche a cooke or fauconer, whome he fyndeth expert, he spareth not to gyue muche wages, with other boūteous rewardes. But of a scholemaister, to whome he wyl cō-mytte his chylde to be fed with learnynge, and instructed in vertue, whose lyfe shalbe the principal monumēt of his name and honour, he neuer maketh further inquery, but where he maye haue a schoolemaister, and with howe littell charge. And if one perchance be founden wel learned, whiche wyll not take peynes to teache without greate salary: he than speaketh nothynge more, or els sayeth, what shall so muche wages be gyuen to a schoolemaister, whiche wolde kepe me two seruantes.

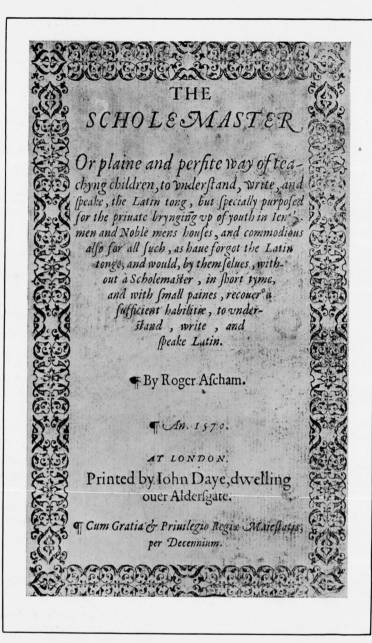

THE
SCHOLEMASTER

Or plaine and perfite way of tea-
chyng children, to vnderstand, write, and
speake, the Latin tong, but specially purposed
for the priuate brynging vp of youth in Ien'-
men and Noble mens houses, and commodious
also for all such, as haue forgot the Latin
tonge, and would, by them selues, without à Scholemaster, in short tyme,
and with small paines, recouer a
sufficient habilitie, to vnderstand, write, and
speake Latin.

By Roger Ascham.

An. 1570.

AT LONDON.
Printed by Iohn Daye, dwelling
ouer Aldersgate.

Cum Gratia & Priuilegio Regiæ Maiestatis,
per Decennium.

TITLE-PAGE OF ASCHAM'S *SCHOLEMASTER*

ROGER ASCHAM

ANOTHER important book for teachers was *The Schole-master*, by Roger Ascham. Roger Ascham lived from 1515 to 1568, spent his childhood in the house of Sir Humphrey Wingfield, was educated at St. John's College, Cambridge, and was made the first Regius Professor of Greek, in 1540. In 1548 Ascham was selected as Princess Elizabeth's tutor. He taught her for two years. He afterwards held various public posts. His earliest work, *Toxophilus*, written in the English tongue (for which he apologizes) emphasizes the importance of archery in education. In *The Scholemasier* he appears as the champion of gentle measures as against "the Rodde" in disciplining children, and, in the teaching of Latin, as the advocate of the method of translation from good authors. I quote from his Preface to the Reader:

> Yet some men, frendly enough of nature, but of small iudgement in learninge, do thinke, I take to moch paines, and spend to moch time, in settinge forth these childrens affaires. But those good men were neuer brought vp in *Socrates* Schole, who saith plainlie, that no man goeth about a more godlie purpose, than he that is mindfull of the good bringing vp, both of hys owne, and other mens children.
>
> Therefore, I trust, good and wise men, will thinke well of this my doing. And of other, that thinke otherwise, I will thinke my selfe, they are but men, to be pardoned for their follie, and pitied for their ignoraunce.
>
> In writing this booke, I haue had earnest respecte to three speciall pointes, trothe of Religion, honestie in liuing, right order in learning.

15

With regard to children's slowness in speaking and writing Latin, Ascham comments as follows:

There is a waie, touched in the first booke of Cicero *De Oratore*, which, wiselie brought into scholes, truely taught, and constantly vsed, would not onely take wholly away this butcherlie feare in making of latines, but would also, with ease and pleasure, and in short time, as I know by good experience, worke a true choice and placing of wordes, a right ordering of sentences, an easie vnderstandyng of the tonge, a readines to speake, a facilitie to write, a true iudgement, both of his owne, and other mens doinges, what tonge so euer he doth vse.

The waie is this. After the three Concordances learned, as I touched before, let the master read vnto hym the Epistles of Cicero, gathered togither and chosen out by Sturmius [German educator (1507–1587)], for the capacitie of children.

First, let him teach the childe, cherefullie and plainlie, the cause, and matter of the letter: then, let him construe it into Englishe, so oft, as the childe may easilie carie awaie the vnderstanding of it: Lastlie, parse it ouer perfitlie. This done thus, let the childe, by and by, both construe and parse it ouer againe: so, that it may appeare, that the childe douteth in nothing, that his master taught him before. After this, the childe must take a paper booke, and sitting in some place, where no man shall prompe him, by him self, let him translate into Englishe his former lesson. Then shewing it to his master, let the master take from him his latin booke, and pausing an houre, at the least, than let the childe translate his owne Englishe into latin againe, in an other paper booke. When the childe bringeth it, turned into latin, the master must compare it with Tullies booke, and laie them both togither: and where the childe doth well, either in chosing, or true placing of Tullies wordes, let the master praise him, and saie here ye do well. For I assure you, there is no such whetstone, to sharpen a good witte and encourage a will to learninge, as is praise.

But if the childe misse, either in forgetting a worde, or in chaunging a good with a worse, or misordering the sen-

16

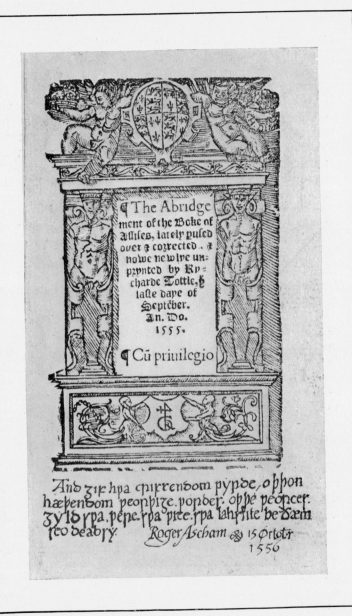

AUTOGRAPH OF ROGER ASCHAM

The writing above his signature is in Anglo-Saxon

tence, I would not haue the master, either froune, or chide with him, if the childe haue done his diligence, and vsed no trewandship therein. For I know by good experience, that a childe shall take more profit of two fautes, ientlie warned of, then of foure thinges, rightly hitt. For than, the master shall haue good occasion to saie vnto him. N. Tullie would haue vsed such a worde, not this: Tullie would haue placed this worde here, not there: would haue vsed this case, this number, this person, this degree, this gender: he would have vsed this moode, this tens, this simple, rather than this compound: this adverbe here, not there: he would haue ended the sentence with this verbe, not with that nowne or participle, &c.

The following quotation shows Ascham's ideas about corporal punishment:

When the great plage was at London, the yeare 1563, the Quenes Maiestie Queene *Elizabeth*, lay at her Castle of Windsore: Where, vpon the 10. day of December, it fortuned, that in Sir *William Cicells* chamber, hir Highnesse Principall Secretarie, there dined togither these personages, M. Secretarie him selfe, Syr *William Peter*, Syr I. *Mason*, D. *Wotton*, Syr *Richard Sackuille* Treasurer of the Exchecker, Syr *Walter Mildmaye* Chauncellor of the Exchecker, M. *Haddon* Master of Requestes, M. *John Astely* Master of the Iewell house, M. *Bernard Hampton*, M. *Nicasius*, and *I*. Of which number, the most part were of hir Maiesties most honourable priuie Counsell, and the reast seruing hir in verie good place. I was glad than, and do reioice yet to remember, that my chance was so happie, to be there that day, in the companie of so manie wise & good men togither, as hardly than could haue bene piked out againe, out of all England beside.

M. Secretarie hath this accustomed maner, though his head be neuer so full of most weightie affaires of the Realme, yet, at diner time he doth seeme to lay them alwaies aside: and findeth euer fitte occasion to taulke pleasantlie of other matters, but most gladlie of some matter of learning: wherein, he will curteslie heare the minde of the meanest at his Table.

Not long after our sitting doune, I haue strange newes brought me, sayth M. Secretarie, this morning, that diuers Scholers of Eaton, be runne awaie from the Schole, for feare of beating. Whereupon, M. Secretarie tooke occasion, to wishe, that some more disdretion were in many Schole-masters, in vsing correction, than commonlie there is. Who many times, punishe rather, the weakenes of nature, than the fault of the Scholer. Whereby, many Scholers, that might else proue well, be driuen to hate learning, before they knowe, what learning meaneth: and so, are made willing to forsake their booke, and be glad to be put to any other kinde of liuing.

M. *Peter*, as one somewhat seuere of nature, said plainlie, that the Rodde onelie, was the sworde, that must keepe, the Schole in obedience, and the Scholer in good order. M. *Wotton*, a man milde of nature, with soft voice, and fewe wordes, inclined to M. Secretaries iudgement, and said, in my opinion, the Scholehouse shoulde be in deede, as it is called by name, the house of playe and pleasure, and not of feare and bondage: and as I do remember, so saith Socrates in one place of Plato. . . . M. *Haddon* was fullie of M. *Peters* opinion, and said, that the best Scholemaster of our time, was the greatest beater, and named the Person. Though, quoth I, it was his good fortune, to send from his Schole vnto the Vniuersitie, one of the best Scholers in deede of all our time, yet wise men do thinke, that that came so to passe, rather, by the great towardnes of the Scholer, than by the great beating of the Master: and whether this be true or no, you your selfe are the best witnes. I said some-what farder in the matter, how, and whie, yong children, were soner allured by loue, than driuen by beating, to atteyne good learning.

Ascham could point to Queen Elizabeth as a good example of the results of the use of his method, as follows:

It is your shame, (I speake to you all, you young Ientle-men of England) that one mayd should go beyond you all, in excellencie of learnyng, and knowledge of diuers tonges. Pointe forth six of the best giuen Ientlemen of this court,

QUEEN ELIZABETH, BY ZUCCARO(?)
Property of the author

and all they together, shew not so much good will, spend
not so much tyme, bestow not so many houres, dayly orderly, & constantly, for the increase of learning & knowledge, as doth the Queenes Maiestie her selfe. Yea I beleue,
that beside her perfit readines, in Latin, Italian, French,
& Spanish, she readeth here now at Windsore more Greeke
euery day, than some Prebendarie of this Chirch doth read
Latin in a whole weeke. And that which is most praise
worthie of all, within the walles of her priuie chamber, she
hath obteyned that excellencie of learnying, to vnderstand,
speake, & write, both wittely with head, and faire with
hand, as scarse one or two rare wittes in both the Uniuersi-
ties haue in many yeares reached vnto. Amongest all the
benefits y^t God hath blessed me with all, next the knowledge
of Christes true Religion, I counte this the greatest, that it
pleased God to call me, to be one poore minister in settyng
forward these excellent giftes of learnyng in this most excellent Prince. Whose onely example, if the rest of our
nobilitie would follow, than might England be, for learnyng
and wisedom in nobilitie, a spectacle to all the world beside.
But see the mishap of men: The best examples haue neuer
such forse to moue to any goodnes, as the bad, vaine, light
and fond, haue to all ilnes.

Another of Ascham's pupils was Lady Jane Grey, about
whom he tells the following anecdote:

And one example, whether loue or feare doth worke more
in a child, for vertue and learning, I will gladly report:
which maie be hard with some pleasure, and followed with
more profit. Before I went into Germanie, I came to
Brodegate in Lecetershire, to take my leaue of that noble
Ladie Iane Grey, to whom I was exceding moch beholdinge.
Hir parentes, the Duke and the Duches, with all the hous-
hould, Gentlemen and Gentlewomen, were huntinge in the
Parke: I founde her, in her Chamber, readinge Phaedon
Platonis in Greeke, and that with as moch delite, as som
ientleman wold read a merie tale in Bocace. After Saluta-
tion and Duty done, with some other Talk, I asked her,
why she would lose such Pastime in the Park? Smiling, she

answered me, "I wist, all their Sport in the Park is but a Shadow to that Pleasure that I find in Plato. Alas! good Folk, they neuer felt what true Pleasure meant." "And how came you, Madam," quoth I, "to this deep Knowledge of Pleasure? and what did chiefly allure you vnto it, seeing not many Women, but very few Men, haue attained there-unto?" "I will tell you," quoth she, "and tell you a Truth which perchance you will maruel at. One of the greatest Benefits that euer God gaue me, is, that he sent me so sharp and seuere Parents, and so gentle a School-master. For when I am in presence either of Father or Mother; whether I speak, keep Silence, sit, stand, or go, eat, drink, be merry, or sad, be sewing, playing, dancing, or doing any Thing else; I must do it, as it were, in such Weight, Measure, and Number, euen so perfectly, as God made the World; or else I am so sharply taunted, so cruelly threatened, yea, presently sometimes with Pinches, Nips, and Bobs, and other ways (which I will not name for the Honour I bear them) so without Measure misorder'd, that I think my self in Hell, till Time come that I must go to Mr. Elmer; who teacheth me so gently, so pleasantly, with such fair Allurements to Learning, that I think all the Time nothing, while I am with him. And when I am called from him, I fall on weeping, because whatsoeuer I do else, but Learning, is full of Grief, Trouble, Fear, and whole misliking vnto me. And thus my Book hath been so much my Pleasure, and bringeth daily to me more Pleasure and more, that in respect of it, all other Pleasures in very deed, be but Trifles and Troubles vnto me."

JUAN LUIS VIVES

IT MAY be of passing interest to contrast with Roger Ascham's idea of the education suitable for Princess Elizabeth the ideas of Princess Mary's instructor as to what she should be taught. Juan Luis Vives was a Spaniard who had studied at Paris, and in 1519 was appointed professor of humanities at Louvain. He was a friend of Erasmus, and was invited to England, where he is supposed to have acted as a tutor for Princess Mary. He lectured on philosophy at Oxford till he fell out of favor by declaring against the divorce of Catherine of Aragon, when he went back to the Continent. His book is called the *Instruction of a christen woman*, and his fear lest the woman be overinstructed is obvious.

In his preface "vnto the moste gracious princesse, Katharine of Englande" (Mary's mother) Vives writes thus:

> I haue beene moued partlie by the holynes and goodnesse of your liuynge, partly by the fauour, loue and zeale that your grace beareth towarde holy studye and learnyng, to write some thyng vnto your good grace, of thinformation and bryngyng vp of a Christen woman: A matter neuer yet entreated of any man, amonge so great plentye and varietee of wittes and writers. For Xenophon and Arystotell geuyng rules of house keepynge, and Plato makynge preceptes of ordrynge the common weale, spake many thynges apperteynyng vnto the womans offyce and dewtie: and sainct Cyprian, sainct Hieronime, sainct Ambrose, and sainct Augustine, haue intreated of maides and wydowes, but in such wyse, that they appere rather to exhorte and counsayle them vnto some kynde of lyuynge, than to instructe and

teache theim. They spende all their speache in the laudes and prayses of chastitie, whyche is a goodly thynge and fyttynge for those great witted and holy men: How be it they wryte but fewe preceptes and rules howe to liue, . . .

Only Chapter IIII is concerned with the "learnyng of maydes", and Vives obviously felt that a very little learning was enough. He says, "I perceiue that learned woman be supected of many", but later refers to a group of ladies "whome their father not content onely to haue thē good and very chast, wold also they shuld be well learned, supposing, that by that meane they shuld be more truely and surely chast", for "a woman sayth Plutarche, geuen vnto lernyng, will neuer delyte in daunsyng".

On another aspect of the teaching of women he writes as follows:

If there maie be founde any holy and well learned womā, I had leauer haue hir to teach them. If there be none, let us chose some man either wel aged, or els very good and vertuous, which hathe a wyfe and that ryght fayre ynough, whome he loueth well, and so shall he not desyre other.

After a long list of the books that ought not to be read, he advises the Bible and the works of Jerome, Cyprian, Augustine, Ambrose, Hilary, Gregory, Plato, Cicero, and Seneca.

Vives wrote *Linguae latinae exercitatio* also, a textbook in dialogue with such subjects as getting up in the morning, getting dressed, morning greetings, going to school, events on the way to school, reading, writing, returning home; in fact, all the events in a boy's daily life.

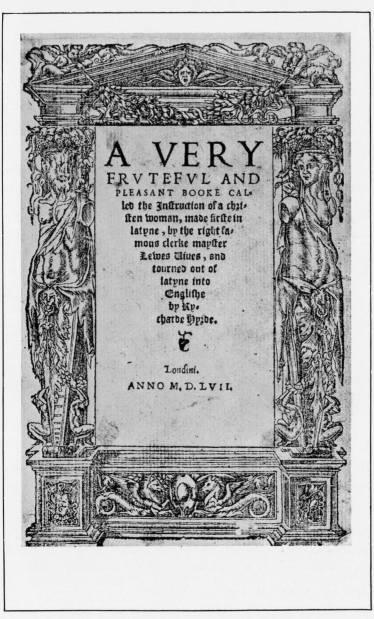

A VERY
FRVTEFVL AND
PLEASANT BOOKE CAL-
led the Instruction of a christen woman, made firste in
latyne, by the right fa-
mous clerke mayster
Lewes Uiues, and
tourned out of
latyne into
Englishe
by Ry-
charde Hyrde.

Londini.
ANNO M.D.LVII.

TITLE-PAGE OF VIVES'S *INSTRVCTION OF A
CHRISTEN WOMAN*

RICHARD MULCASTER

RICHARD MULCASTER was the headmaster of the Merchant Taylors' School, where Spenser is supposed to have been one of his pupils. It is often thought that Mulcaster is the original of Holofernes in *Love's Labour's Lost*.

Loues Labour's lost, Act IV

Enter *Dull, Holofernes*, the *Pedant* and *Nathaniel*.

Nat. Very reuerent sport truely, and done in the testimony of a good conscience.

Ped. The Deare was (as you know) sanguis in blood, ripe as a Pomwater, who now hangeth like a Iewell in the eare of *Celo* the skie; the welken the heauen, and anon falleth like a Crab on the face of *Terra*, the soyle, the land, the earth.

Curat. Nath. Truly M. *Holofernes*, the epythithes are sweetly varied like a scholler at the least: but sir I assure ye, it was a Bucke of the first head.

Hol. Sir *Nathaniel, haud credo.*

Dul. 'Twas not a *haud credo*, 'twas a Pricket.

Hol. Most barbarous intimation: yet a kinde of insinuation, as it were *in via*, in way of explication *facere*: as it were replication, or rather *ostentare*, to show as it were his inclination after his vndressed, vnpolished, vneducated, vnpruned, vntrained, or rather vnlettered, or ratherest vnconfirmed fashion, to insert againe my *haud credo* for a Deare.

Dul. I said the Deare was not a *haud credo,*'twas a Pricket.

Hol. Twice sod simplicitie, *bis coctus*, O thou monster Ignorance, how deformed doost thou looke.

Nath. Sir hee hath neuer fed of the dainties that are bred in a booke. he hath not eate paper as it were: he hath not drunke inke. His intellect is not replenished, hee is onely an animall, onely sensible in the duller parts: . . .

26

However, in spite of what some think of Mulcaster's pompous speech, he was a man with good theories of teaching. In his book *Positions* (1581) he says that he would have girls receive as good an education as boys. While he recommended that they should "set not yong *maidens* to publike grammer scholes", it was only because this was "a thing not vsed in my countrie".

He suggested special training to enable men to teach.

He wishes the child to be "perfect, and ready, in both the English and the Latin tongue verie long before he dreame of his grammar". Formerly it was doubtful whether the child should read Latin or English first, and while his religion was in Latin he read Latin first. Now that his religion is in English he must read that first.

". . . our English tung . . . is of small reatch, it stretcheth no further than this Ilād of ours naie not there over all". He insists that it be cultivated and used as a vehicle of learning.

The chapter-headings give a good idea of the book.

Cap. 4.

What time were best for the childe to begin to learne. What matters some of the best writers handle eare they determine this question. Of letters and libertie, whervnto the parentes are subiect in setting their children to schoole. Of the difference of wittes and bodies in children. That exercise must be ioyned with the booke, as the schooling of the bodie.

Cap. 5.

What thinges they be, wherin children are to be trained, eare they passe to the Grammar. That parentes, and maisters ought to examine the naturall abilities in children, whereby they become either fit, or unfit, to this, or that kinde of life. The three naturall powers in children, Witte

POSITIONS

VVHERIN THOSE PRI-
MITIVE CIRCVMSTANCES

BE EXAMINED, WHICH ARE NE-
CESSARIE FOR THE TRAINING
vp of children, either for skill in their
booke, or health in their bodie.

VVRITTEN by RICHARD MVLCASTER, *maſter
of the ſchoole erected in London anno.* 1561. *in the pa-
riſh of Sainct Laurence Povvntneie, by the vvorſhipfull
companie of the merchaunt tailers of the ſaid citie.*

Imprinted at London by Thomas Vautrollier
for Thomas Chare.
1581

TITLE-PAGE OF MULCASTER'S *TRAINING VP OF CHILDREN*

to conceiue by, Memorie to retaine by, Discretion to discerne by. Of Reading, Writing, Drawing, Musicke by voice, and instrument: and that they be the principall principles, to traine vp the minde in. A generall answere to all obiections, which arise against any, or all of these.

Cap. 6.

Of exercises and training the body. How necessarie a thing exercise is. What health is, and how it is maintained: what sicknesse is, how it cometh, and how it is preuented. What a parte exercise playeth in the maintenaunce of health. Of the student and his health. That all exercises though they stirre some one parte most, yet helpe the whole bodie.

The next twenty-nine chapters are devoted to exercise.

Cap. 36.

That both yong boyes, and yong maidens are to be put to learne. Whether all boyes be to be set to schoole. That to many learned be burdenous: to few to bare: wittes well sorted ciuill: missorted seditious. That all may learn to write and reade without daunger. The good of choice, the ill of confusiō. The childrē which are set to learne hauing either rich or poore friends, what order & choice is to be used in admitting either of them to learne. Of the time to chuse.

Cap. 37.

The meanes to restraine the ouerflowing multitude of scholers. The cause why euery one desireth, to haue his childe learned. . . .

Cap. 38.

That yong maidens are to be set to learning, which is proued by the custome of our countrie, by our duetie towards them, by their naturall abilitie, and by the worthie effectes of such as haue bene well trained. The ende whereunto their education serueth, which is the cause why and how much they learne. Which of them are to learne. When they are to beginne to learne: What and how much they may learne. Of whom and where they ought to be taught.

The book has in all forty-five chapters.

Mulcaster's second book, *The Elementarie*, was published in 1582, and remained for two hundred and fifty years the first English treatise on instruction.

Foster Watson, in *English Grammar Schools to 1660*, says,

> Briefly the *Elementarie* may be described as the demand for a *liberal* education from the very earliest stages of school instruction. Mulcaster attempts to show how to "handle the young wit: how to join exercise of the body with principles of training for the mind". He lays down a method for the teacher to teach the necessary subjects of the curriculum, which must include music and drawing. He also instructs the child as to his best methods of learning, tells him what to learn by heart, and what to study. He considers special directions, even down to details, necessary for both teachers and scholars, because "the elementary master is not commonly the cunningest and the elementary scholar is under twelve years of age". With the course of training described in the *Elementarie* Mulcaster maintains that the child "shall learne the tongue (i. e. Latin) sooner, and do more between twelve and sixteen, than from seven to seventeen, if he begins without this train".

Mulcaster had dedicated his first book to Elizabeth. He dedicated his second to Leicester, saying,

> as the considerations, which enforced me to offer hir maiestie the first frutes of my publik writing, were exceeding great, so those reasons, which induce me now to present to your honor, this my second labor, be not verie small. . . . I handle speciallie in it the right writing of our English tung.

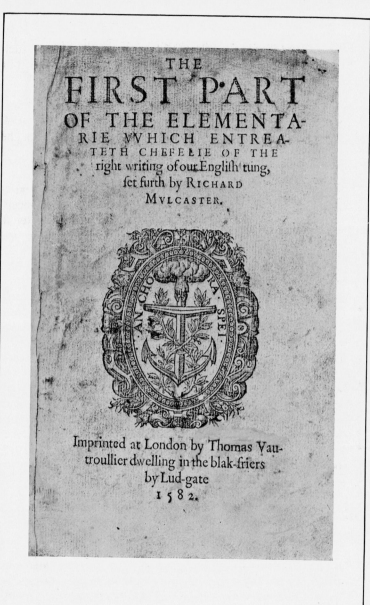

THE
FIRST P·ART
OF THE ELEMENTA-
RIE VVHICH ENTREA-
TETH CHEFELIE OF THE
right writing of our English tung,
fet furth by RICHARD
MVLCASTER.

Imprinted at London by Thomas Vau-
troullier dwelling in the blak-friers
by Lud-gate
1 5 8 2.

TITLE-PAGE OF THE FIRST PART OF THE *ELEMENTARIE*

And in the peroration he discourses of English as follows:

For the generall penning in the *English* tung, I must
nedes saie this much, that in som points of handling by
the tung, there is none more excellent then ours is. As in
the teaching kinde no work memorie with delite, like the
old leonine verses, which run in rime, it doth admit such
daliance, with the letter, as I know not anie. And in that
kinde, where remembrance is the end, it is without blame,
tho otherwise not, if it com in to often, and bewraie affec-
tation not sound but followed. In the staie of speche, &
strong ending, it is verie forcible and stout, bycause of the
monosyllab, which is the chefe ground & ordinarie pitch
of both our pen & tung. For fine translating in pithie terms,
either pere to, or passing the foren quiknesse, I find it
wonderfull pliable, and redie to discharge a quik conceit,
in verie few words. For close deliuerie of much matter in
not manie words generallie, it will do as much in the
primitiue vtterance as in anie translation.

betle.	birch	bleak	bodie
betroth	bird	blear	bodkin
betrothed	birder	bleareie	boisterqus
betraie	birdlime	bleat	bold
better	birt	bled	bolt
betwene	birth	blede	bolster
beuie	biſſie	blek	bolstered
beware	biſcot	bleke	bone
bewail	bisket } Enſtran.	blemish	bonet
bewitch Deriuat	biſhop	blend	bond
bewraie	bit	blew	bondage
bewrap	bite	blind	book
beyond	biter	blindneſſe	boot
Biace	bitterlie	blindfild	bootie
bib	bitterneſſe	blink	bore
bible	bittor	blinks	borne
bible } Diſtinct.	Blab	blirt	borrow
bich	blabberlip	bliſſe	bo
bichrie	blade	bliſſing	boſom
bid	bladder	blister	boſſe
bide	blake	blok	boſte
biden	blak	blokkish	boſting } e, Orignal
big	blakkish	blood,	bot
bigamie Enſtran.	blame	bloodie	bote
bigger	blamewhorthie	bloſſom	both
biggin	blane	blot	bott
bigneſſe	blanche	blote	botethan
bikker	blank	blow	bothe
bikkering	blanket	blown	botcher.
bikring Contract.	blaſe	blubber	botle
bill	blaſing	blunt	bottom
bile	blaſpheme	blur	bottomleſſe
billet	blasfeam } Enfr.	blush	bountie
billement Enſtran	blaſphemie	bluster	bountifull
billing	blaſt	blustering	boun
bin	blaſted	bluſtring Com	boult
bind	bleath	Bob	bourd
binding	bleacht Con ract.	bobbins	bourder
bing	bleaching	bode	bour
			bouth

LVDVS LITERARIVS:

OR,

THE GRAMMAR SCHOOLE;

SHEWING HOW TO PRO-

ceede from the first entrance into learning, to the highest perfection required in the GRAMMAR SCHOOLES, with ease, certainty and delight both to Masters and Schollars; onely according to our common Grammar, and ordinary Classicall Authours:

BEGVN TO BE SOVGHT OVT AT THE desire of some worthy fauourers of learning, by searching the experiments of sundry most profitable Schoolemasters and other learned, and confirmed by tryall:

Intended for the helping of the younger sort of Teachers, and of all Schollars, with all other desirous of learning; for the perpetuall benefit of Church and Common-wealth.

It offereth it selfe to all to whom it may doe good, or of whom it may receiue good to bring it towards perfection.

Χρὴ Μουσῶν θεράποντα καὶ ἄγγελον, εἴ τι περισσὸν
εἰδείη σοφίης, μὴ φθονερὸν τελέθειν,
ἀλλὰ τὰ μὲν μῶσθαι, τὰ δὲ δεικνύναι, ἄλλα δὲ ποιεῖν.
τί σφιν χρήσηται μοῦνος ἐπιστάμενος. *Theognis.*

Nullum munus Reipub. affere maius meliúsue possumus, quam si doceamus atq; erudimus iuuentutem. Cic. 3. de Diuin.

Quærendi defatigatio turpis est, cum id quod quæritur sit pulcherrimum. 2. de Finibus.

LONDON,
Printed for THOMAS MAN. 1612.

TITLE-PAGE OF BRINSLEY'S *GRAMMAR SCHOOLE*

JOHN BRINSLEY

JOHN BRINSLEY the elder took his M. A. at Cambridge, in 1588, and was headmaster of the public school at Ashby-de-la-Zouch, where he taught, among others, William Lilly, the astrologer, who says of him,

> Upon Trinity Sunday 1613, my father had me to Ashby-de-la-Zouch to be instructed by one Mr. John Brinsley; one in those times of great abilities for instruction of youth in the Latin and Greek tongues; he was very severe in his life and conversation, and did breed up many scholars for the universities. In religion he was a strict puritan, not conformable wholly to the ceremonies of the church of England.

Though Brinsley wrote his *Grammar Schoole* in 1612, still the conditions had changed little since Shakespeare's day, and we need not feel that what he says does not apply. He has a preface "To the louing Reader", beginning, "Cvrteous Reader, who tenderest the poore Countrey Schooles, for which this labour hath beene vndertaken". In reading this book we may therefore feel that we have a schoolmaster's testimony as to what would be taught in such a school as that at Stratford.

The book consists of a discourse between two school-masters, Spoudeus ("Earnest") and Philoponvs ("Lover of Toil"). Spoudeus seeks counsel of the other, for, he says, he has "so long laboured in this moyling and drudging life", that he is "vtterly wearie" of his place, and his life is a "continuall burden vnto" him.

Philoponvs replies that he has found a way of teaching which makes the work a very different thing:

> I doe plainely see such a change, that now I doe not only labour in my place vsually without griefe, or any wearinesse at all, but that I can take ordinarilie more true delight and pleasure in following my children . . . then anie one can take in following hawkes and hounds.

Philoponvs' plan was to fit the child for the university at fifteen years of age, and therefore to begin school not later than at five years, for he can learn "shrewdnesse" and "hurtful" things before five, and might as well be learning things that are profitable; there is danger, also, of his getting so fond of play that he will be unwilling to study; he is most pliant at this age, and it is well to save time in preparation for the university. Then, too, he will become accustomed to school early, and so form good habits. He also says "Let the schoole be made vnto them a place of play."

Philoponvs outlines a quick method of learning to read in one year. First, to teach the child to pronounce every letter plainly, fully and distinctly; then, besides saying the alphabet forward and backward, to have him pick out letters at random. Drill him in spelling, first syllables of two letters, then more. Repeat again and again those which he spells wrong. Be sure to pronounce correctly the words which you wish spelled.

Next, for reading, he recommends the following books:

> the primer,— and read it a second time also,
> the Psalms, in metre since this makes the reading
>   pleasant and easy,
> the Testament,
> the "Schoole of Vertue" (also in metre), and
> the "Schoole of good manners".

With respect to the teaching of English, complaints are made by parents that children forget how to read English in learning Latin. The child must learn to use his native tongue. He should read over English "parts" [parts of speech?], use "Lillies rules" in books of construing, translate into English daily all the school authors, and have daily practice in writing, translation, familiar letters to friends, repetition of fables in English, and taking notes on sermons.

He must study to express whatever he construes "in variety of the finest phrase, who can giue the best", and let him study the history of the Bible.

When beginning numbers, the child should be trained to read numbers readily and be able to write them, both letters (that is, Roman numerals) and figures; if more is wanted "seeke Records Arithmetique, or other like Authors and set them to the Cyphering schoole".

He feels that more attention should be paid to writing.

> For many of the best Schollars, haue beene wont to write very ill; in so much, as it hath beene a receiued opinion, as you know, amongst very many, That a good Schollar can hardly be a good pen-man. Moreouer you shall finde very fewe good writers in Grammar Schooles; vnlesse eyther they haue beene taught by Scriueners, or be themselues maruellous apt hereunto, and very rare, or where the Master doth apply himselfe chiefly to teach to write.

Brinsley devotes a whole chapter to method, summing up in these words, "Most shortly, these three are almost all in all; good copies, continual eying them wel, a delight in writing."

Of religion he says

> How schollars maie bee taught . . .
> 1. To be acquainted with all the grounds of religion and chief histories of the Bible.

2. So to take the Sermons, at least for all the substance both for doctrines, proofes, vses; and after to make a rehearsall of them.

3. Euery one to begin to conceiue and answere the seuerall points of the Sermons, euen from the lowest formes.

Every Saturday half an hour or more is to be spent in learning and answering the catechism. The master should make all the words plain to the "least childe" amongst them.

Also he must make all take notes of sermons, even the very lowest, at least three or four, such as "Without God we can do nothing", and monitors must see that all be attentive to the preacher.

"Let them set down the Text or a part of it, and every doctrine."

In the highest forms, he should cause them to set down all the sermons (that is, "substance" and "effect"), distinguishing the several parts by letters or figures. If he thinks best, let him have them translate it "into a good Latine stile" the next morning, or read the English into Latin, *ex tempore.*

The benefit of all this is that, besides increasing their knowledge, it will keep them from "playing, talking, sleeping and all other disorders in the Church".

For other days than Sunday, have prayer and thanksgiving morning and evening, and read every night a piece of M. Paget's *History of the Bible.*

As to manners, religion will teach them good manners.

The master can get some help on manners and civility from the authors read, that is, Cato, Cicero's *Offices, Qui mihi, Sententiae pueriles,* etc., and also in a little book translated from the French, *The Schoole of good manners,* or *The new Schoole of vertue.*

The following topics are treated in the book:

Accidence: Grammar: Construing: Parsing: "Making" Latin: Epistles imitating Tully and how to write "letters to our friends in English accordinglie": "Theames" (themes): Versifying ("How to enter to make verses with delight and certainty, without bodging"): Manner of examining and correcting exercises: Grammar: "Rhetoricke": Pronunciation: Speaking Latin purely and readily: "Greeke": Hebrew: Religion: Morals: Qualifications of the schoolmaster, of the Usher: Government: Preferments: Punishments: School-times: Intermissions: Recreations: Evils of absence: Unthankfulness of parents: What scholars are to be sent to Universities.

THE
ENGLISH
SCHOOL-MASTER.

Teaching all his Scholars , of what age foever, the moſt eaſy, ſhort, and perfect order of diſtinct Reading , and true Writing our Engliſh-tongue , that hath ever yet been known or publiſhed by any.

And further alſo, teacheth a direct courſe, how any unskilful perſon may eaſily both underſtand any hard Engliſh words which they ſhall in Scriptures, Sermons, or elſe-where hear or read, and alſo b: made able to uſe the ſame aptly themſelves ; and generally whatſoever is neceſſary to be known for the *Engliſh* Speech; ſo that he which hath this Book only, needeth to buy no other to make him fit from his Letters to the *Grammar-School*, for an *Apprentice*, or any other private uſe, ſo far as concerneth *Engliſh*. And therefore it is made not only for Children, though the firſt Book be mere childiſh for them; but alſo for all other , eſpecially for thoſe that are ignorant in the *Latin* Tongue.

In the next Page the *School-Maſter* hangeth forth his Table to the view of all beholders, ſetting forth ſome of the chief Commodities of his Profeſſion.

Deviſed for thy ſake that wanteſt any part of this skill, by *Edward Coote*, Maſter of the Free-School in Saint *Edmonds-Bury*.

Peruſed and approved by publick Authority ; and now the 47 time Imprinted: with certain Copies to Write by, at the end of this book, added.

Printed by *R. Roberts* for the Company of *Stationers*. 1692.

TITLE-PAGE OF COOTE'S *ENGLISH SCHOOL-MASTER*

EDWARD COOTE

FOR more than a hundred years *The English School-Master*, by Edward Coote, was a popular elementary book. At the date of the edition illustrated (1692) the book had been printed forty-seven times. There was an edition as early as 1596. It begins with the alphabet, and contains chapters on reading, grammar, and the catechism, prayers for various occasions, a dictionary, arithmetic, and specimens of printing. One of the reading selections, entitled "The School-Master to his Schollar", shows the ideals of this author:

> My Child and Schollar, take good heed
> unto the Words that here are set,
> And see thou do accordingly,
> or else besure thou shalt be beat.
>
> First, I command thee, God to serve,
> then to thy Parents duty yield,
> Unto all Men be courteous,
> and mannerly in town and field.

Coote shows in his preface that he expects to appeal to the lower classes as well as to the educated:

> I am now therefore to direct my speech unto the unskilful, which desire to make use of it for their own private benefit, and to such men and women of Trade, as Tailors, Weavers, Shopkeepers, Sempsters, and such others, as have undertaken the charge of teaching others . . . thou mayest sit on thy shop board, at thy Loom, or at thy Needle, and never hinder thy work to hear thy Scholars, after once thou hast made this little book familiar to thee.

41

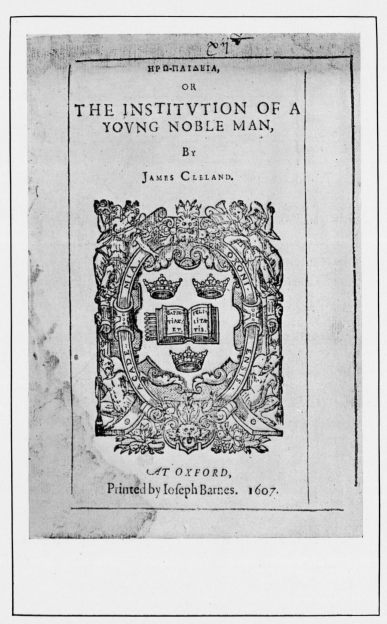

TITLE-PAGE OF CLELAND'S *INSTITVTION*
OF A YOVNG NOBLE MAN

JAMES CLELAND

JAMES CLELAND dedicates his book *The Institution of a Young Noble Man* to Prince Charles, Duke of York, the second son of King James. The matter of his treatise is set forth in the list of chapters, as follows:

THE SUBJECT, AND OR–
der of these six Bookes.

The first booke sheweth the dutie of Parents towards their children, containing 9. Chapters.

D. to my Lord Hay.

The second booke adviseth Tutors of their duty, containing 12. Chapters.

D. to Mr. Newton, and to Mr. Mourray.

The third booke sheweth a young Noble mans duty towards God, containing 3. Chapters.

D. to my Lord Gordon.

The fourth booke sheweth a young Noblemans duety towards his Parents, and Tutor, containing 8. Chapt.

D. to Sir John Harington.

The fifth booke sheweth a young Noble mans duty in Civil Conversation, containing 31. Chapt.

D. to Mr. Francis, and to Mr. John, Stewarts.

The sixth booke pointeth out a young Noblemans way in travelling, containing 5. Chapt.

D. to my Lord of Essex.

Not very much of the volume is spent on book-learning, but Chapter Three of the Fourth Book is headed "How profitable learning is, and how hurtful ignorance is vnto a Noble man", and continues thus:

False and fantastical opinion preuaileth so against reason now a daies, that ignorance is thought an essential marke of

43

a Noble mā by many. If a yoūg childe loueth not an Hawke and a Dogge while he sitteth vpon his nurses lap, it is a token, saie they, he degenerates. Such is the miserie & blindnes of this vnhappie age, that manie growing in yeares professe nothing more than scoffing at learning & the professors thereof, in calling them al *clerks* or *pedants*. If they perceiue anie Noble man better disposed to learning then themselues, presentlie after a scorning manner they wil baptize him with the name of Philosopher: haue he a compasse and a rule in his studie, then hee is an Astrologian; can he make halfe a sonnet, hee is a rimer. Notwithstanding learning only putteth a difference betwixte men, as reason maketh vs better then the brut beasts.

III. *Courses of Study in Shakespeare's Day*

THE types of textbooks that were in use in the country schools in Shakespeare's day are suggested by the following courses of study:

THE FREE GRAMMAR SCHOOL, ST. BEES, CUMBERLAND, 1583

English	*Prose*
A-B-C in English	Æsop's Fables
Catechism	Cicero
Psalter and Book of Common Prayer	Sallust
New Testament	Justinus
Queen's Grammar with accidence	Cæsar
Small Catechism in Latin	
Confabulationes Pueriles	

Verse

Quintus Curtius	Terence	Horace
Disticha Moralia Catonis	Virgil	Ovid

HOOLE'S LIST FOR THE ROTHERHAM GRAMMAR SCHOOL

Accidence, Sententiae Pueriles.

Lily's Grammar, Cato's Maxims, Pueriles Confabulationes, Colloquia of Corderius.

Grammar, Latin Testament, Æsop's Fables, Dialogues of Casteleo, Eclogues of Mantuanus, Colloquies of Helvicius.

BRINSLEY'S LIST

Lily, accidence, construing, Sententiae Pueriles, Cato, Corderius's Dialogues, Æsop's Fables, Tully's Epistles, Tully's Offices, De Amicitia, De Senectute, Ovid's Metamorphoses, Virgil.

Upper School: Plautus, Horace, Persius, Juvenal: pupils writing themes, verses.

45

THE EDUCATION OF SHAKESPEARE

John Lyon's Course of Study

John Lyon, founder of Harrow, in 1561 prescribed the following as his course of study:

In the lower three forms, Latin grammar, Cicero, Cato, Terence, Ovid. In the fourth form, Virgil, Cæsar, Cicero, Livy, Demosthenes, Socrates, Hesiod, with verses and themes.

In 1785, two hundred and twenty-four years after, the only change in the Harrow course is more Greek and verse-writing; and in 1829, nearly fifty years later, we find modern and ancient history, Euclid, and vulgar fractions. In 1837 the study of mathematics was made compulsory, and in 1857 modern languages were introduced.

Mr. Talbot, Lord Lieutenant of Glamorganshire, speaks as follows of his experience at Harrow in 1852:

It was in my time absolute heresy for a master to attempt to teach anything but Greek and Latin. Mathematics and French were not allowed. It is quite true that there was a French master, but he lived the life of a dog, and there were, also, writing and arithmetic masters, but whenever they appeared they were received with hallooing and hooting.

IV. *The Textbooks of Shakespeare's Day*

I HAVE several textbooks that were in use when Shakespeare was in school. I reproduce pages and quote briefly from a few of them. If anyone wishes to learn further about the possibility that these particular books were studied by Shakespeare, I refer him to H. R. D. Anders's *Shakespeare's Books*, an interesting and elaborate compilation of quotations from Shakespeare's writings which are either allusions to certain books or quoted directly from them, and which seem to me very interesting evidence.

We come at last to the school career of Shakespeare. Presumably he went to school when he was six or seven years old, or about 1571, and he may have stayed till he was about fifteen. If so, he would be taught, according to Anders, for two years by Walter Roche, five years by Samuel Hunt, and possibly three by Thomas Jenkins, masters of the school at Stratford, all university men. The first book put into his hand was a hornbook.

The typical hornbook was a piece of metal or wood to which was fastened a parchment setting forth the alphabets, large and small, vowels and syllables, the exorcism, and the Lord's Prayer; over this was tacked a piece of transparent horn, so the child would not stain it. The first line began with a cross, and was called the Christcross-row, crisscross-row, or crossrow. The exorcism was to be learned because every boy was supposed to be more or less full of the devil.

47

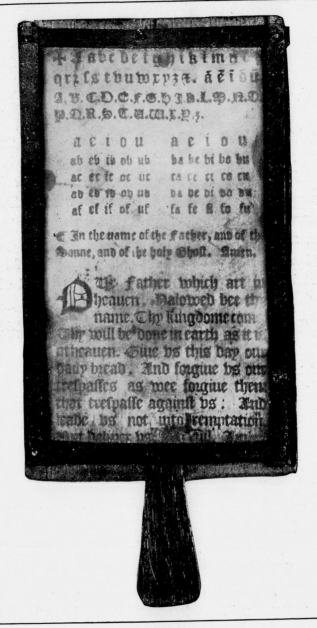

A TYPICAL HORNBOOK

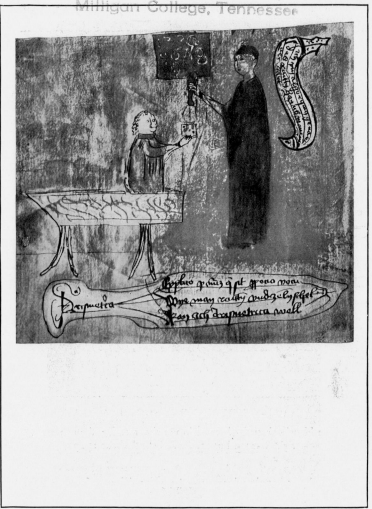

HORNBOOK DRAWN IN A MANUSCRIPT OF SACROBOSCO

This picture of a hornbook was made from a drawing in a fifteenth-century manuscript on science by one Sacrobosco. The scribe, or possibly some student of the volume, grew tired of his work, and amused himself by drawing a schoolroom scene on a blank half-page. The lesson is on algorisms, and the book has Hindu numerals instead of the alphabet. The date of the earliest use of the hornbook is unknown. Foster Watson says that Tuer found no hornbook earlier than 1450, but that it was probably used much earlier. The author's library has nearly forty hornbooks of various kinds

METAL HORNBOOKS

The Hornbook at the left was in use about 1664; the one at the
right was used at St. Paul's School about 1729

In Shakespeare's plays are two familiar references to the
hornbook:

> *Brag.* Mounsier, are you not lettred?
> *Page.* Yes, yes, he teaches boyes the Horne-booke:
> What is Ab speld backward with the horn on his head?
> (*Loues Labour's lost,* IV (1 F.) [i.e. V], line 49)
> *Clar.* . . . He hearkens after Prophesies and Dreames,
> And from the Crosse-row pluckes the letter G:
> And sayes, a Wizard told him, that by G,
> His issue disinherited should be. (*Richard III,* I, line 56)

MANUSCRIPT OF A PRIMER OF THE FIFTEENTH CENTURY

A PAGE FROM THE PETYT PRIMER

PRIMERS

AFTER the hornbook, boys studied the primer. The first page of the primer was taken from the hornbook, as illustrated by the manuscript, on vellum, of a primer of the fifteenth century, in English, that I have in my collection.

One of the first primers was printed in England by John Petyt. It is not in my collection, but in the library of Emmanuel College, Cambridge. I reproduce a facsimile edited by E. S. Schuckbergh in 1889. It was the forerunner of Henry VIII's Primer, of which I have the edition of 1545.

Henry VIII required this primer to be used in all the schools in England, and doubtless it was still in use in Shakespeare's day.

In the "inivnction" Henry VIII says,

> Emong the manifolde businesse, and moste weightie affaires appartainyng to our regall authoritee and office, wee muche tenderyng the youthe of our realmes, (whose good educacion and vertuouse bryngyng vp redouneth moste highly to the honoure and praise of almightie God) for diuers good consideracions, and specially for that the youthe by diuers persones are taught the Pater noster, the Aue Maria, Crede, and ten commaundementes all in Latin and not in Englishe, by meanes whereof thesame are not brought vp in the knoweledge of their faith, dutie and obedience, wherein no Christen persone ought to bee ignoraunt . . . And furthermore, wee strightly charge and commaunde aswell all and singulare our subiectes and sellers of bokes, as also al scholemasters and teachers of young children within this our realme and other our dominions, as thei

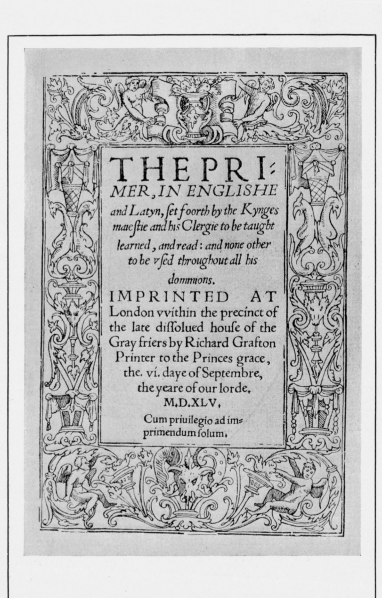

TITLE-PAGE OF THE PRIMER OF HENRY VIII

AN INIVNCTION CEVEN

by the Kyng our foуereigne lordes moste ex=
cellente maiestie for the autorisyng and
establishyng the vse of this
Primer.

HENRY THE EIGHT BY
the grace of God kyng of Englād,
Fraunce, and Irelande, defendour
of the faithe and of the churche of
Englande and also of Irelande in
pearth the supreme hedde. To all
and singulare our subiectes aſwel
Archebiſhoppes, Biſhoppes, dea=
nes, Archedeacons, Prouoſtes, perſones, vicares, cu=
rates, prieſtes, and all other of the Cleargie: as alſo all
eſtates and degrees of the laie fee, and teachers of
pouthe within any our realmes, dominions, and coun=
tries gretyng. Emong the manifolde buſineſſe, and
moſte weightie affaires appartainyng to our regall
authoritee and office, wee muche tenderyng the pouthe
of our realmes, (whoſe good educacion and vertuouſe
bryngyng vp redouneth moſte highly to the honoure
and praiſe of almightie God) for diuers good conſide=
tacions, and ſpecially for that the pouthe by diuers
perſones are taught the Pater noster, the Aue Maria,
Crede, and ten commaundementes all in Latin and
not in Engliſhe, by meanes whereof theſame are not
brought vp in the knoweledge of their faith, dutie and

C.i. obedience

entende to haue our fauour and auoyde our displeasure by the contrary, that immediately after this our saied Primer is published and imprinted, that thei ne any of theim, bye, sell, occupie, vse, nor teache priuily or apertly any other Primer either in Englishe or latin, then this, now by vs published . . .

This copy of the primer belonged to Thomas Thirlby, Bishop of Westminster under Henry VIII, who was one of the commission sent to examine Queen Catherine Howard on a charge which ultimately led to her execution. How much she confessed to them is not very clear, but that she "acknowledged her offences against God the King and the nation" is a matter of history.

In the calendar in this book Thirlby has noted that he was deposed from the bishopric of Ely on July 5, 1559 (by Elizabeth, for his refusal to take the oath of supremacy), and sent to the Tower on June 3, 1560, and that on June 4, 1561, St. Paul's spire was struck by lightning and burnt, on "Corpus Christi even".

THE BIBLE

THEN followed the Bible. The edition in use was the
Geneva Bible, sometimes called the "Breeches Bible"
because in the third chapter of Genesis it says, "and they
sewed fig-leaves together and made themselves breeches".
This edition was printed by the refugees who fled to the
Continent during the reign of Queen Mary.

Later the refugees came back to England, and the Bible
was studied. In 1559 Queen Elizabeth ordered the Bible and
the Paraphrases of Erasmus in English on the Gospels to
be read in every church.

INJUNCTIONS OF COMMISSIONERS TO WINCHESTER COLLEGE,
1547

From henceforth the Bible shall be daily read in English,
distinctly and apertly, in the midst of the Hall, above the
Hearth where the fire is made both at Dinner and Supper.
That as well all the scholars and other coming to the School,
being able to buy the New Testament in English and Latin,
shall provide for the same betwixt this and Christmas next
coming, to the intent that they may every Sunday and other
Holy Day exercise themselves holie in reading thereof;
setting apart all other exercises of profane authors, and
that the warden and school master or such as the warden
in his absence shall appoint shall diligently from time to
time examine them of their exercise in his behalf.

THE BIBLE

AND

HOLY SCRIPTVRES

CONTEYNED IN

THE OLDE AND NEWE

Teſtament.

TRANSLATED ACCOR-

ding to the Ebrue and Greke, and conferred with

the beſt tranſlations in diuers langages.

WITH MOSTE PROFITABLE ANNOTA-

tions vpon all the hard places, and other things of great

importance as may appeare in the Epiſtle to the Reader.

FEARE YE NOT, STAND ETIL. AND BEHOLDE

the ſaluacion of the Lord, which he wil ſhewe to you this day. Exod. 14, 13.

HEB 12: 7, 11.

THE LORD SHAL FIGHT FOR YOU: THEREFORE

holde you your peace. Exod. 14, ver. 14.

AT GENEVA.

PRINTED BY ROULAND HALL

M·D·LX·

TITLE-PAGE OF THE GENEVA BIBLE

ALEXANDER NOWELL

Reproduced by permission of the Bodleian Library

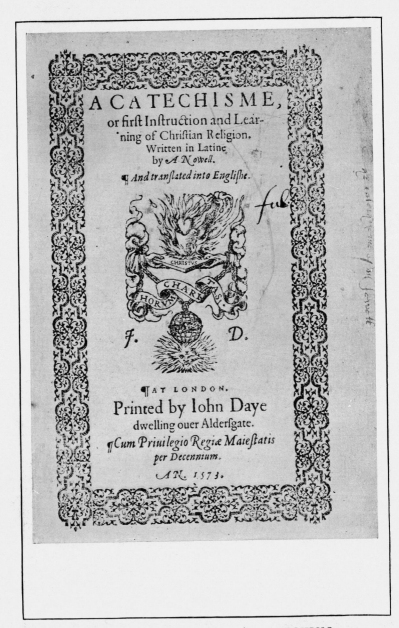

TITLE-PAGE OF NOWELL'S CATECHISM

THE CATECHISM

ONE of the duties of all teachers was to expound religion, as one of the chief reasons for going to school was to understand it. The child's first instruction in his creed was found in the catechism. Catechisms were dialogues in the form of questions and answers which, when explained by the teacher and learned by heart by the child, gave him his first inkling of doctrinal matters.

THE HARROW RULES OF 1580

Every scholar shall be taught to say the Lord's Prayer, the Articles of faith, the Ten Commandments, and other chief parts of the Catechism and principal points of Christian religion, in English first, and after in Latin, and on Sundays and holidays, the Master shall read a Lecture to all, or the most part of the Scholars, which he shall think meet to hear thereof out of Calvin or Nowell's Catechism...

STATUTES OF RIVINGTON SCHOOL, 1556

On Saturdays and Holy Day eves, the Usher shall exercise his younger sort in learning their short Catechism in English in the Common Book, and the same days to all sorts the Master shall read Mr: Nowell's or Calvin's Catechism, taught in Calvin's Institutions, willing the elder sort both to learn it by heart, and examine them briefly the next day after, when they come to School again, before they go to other things, how they can say it, and shall commend them that have done well, and encourage others to do the like.

Alexander Nowell (1507–1602) was educated at Brasenose College, Oxford, where he is said to have roomed with

THE
Catechisme, or maner
to teache Children
the Christian
Religion.

⁋ Made by the excellent
doctor and pastor in Christes Churche Ihon Calvin.
wherein the minister demaun-
deth the Question, and
the Childe maketh
Aunswere.

EPHES. 2.
The doctrine of the Apostles and
Prophetes is the foundation
of Christes Churche.

Imprinted at London, by
Ihon Kyngston.

1580.

TITLE-PAGE OF CALVIN'S CATECHISM

This is the most famous of all catechisms and the basis of all. The
illustration is a pen-drawing from the edition of 1580

Hat is the principall and chiefest ende of mannes life?
The Childe.
To knowe God.

M. What moueth thee to saie so?

C. Because he hath created vs, and placed vs in this worlde, to sette forthe his glorie in vs, and it is good reason, that we imploie our whole life to his glory, seyng he is the beginnyng and fountaine thereof. *whereunto man was created & made.*

M. What is the the chiefest felicitie of man?
C. Euen the self same, I meane to knowe God, & to haue his glory shewed forth in vs. *The greatest felicitie that man can attaine to.*

M. Why doest thou call this, mannes chief felicitie?
C. Because that without it our condition, or state were more miserable, then the state of brute beastes.

M. Hereby then we maie euidently se, that there can no suche miserie come vnto man, as not to liue in the knowledge of God.
C. That is most certaine.

M. But what is the true, and right knowledge of God?
C. When a man so knoweth God, that he giueth hym due honour. *The true knowledge of God.*

A.y. M. Whiche

FIRST PAGE OF CALVIN'S CATECHISM

JOHN CALVIN

John Foxe. He was master of Westminster School from 1543 to 1560. He became Dean of St. Paul's, and held the office for forty-two years. He is supposed to have written the catechism that stood in the Order of the Confirmation in the Prayer Book of 1549. In 1570, early in Elizabeth's reign, he wrote a large catechism, and in the same year a "middle" catechism "for simple curates". Both were translated into English by T. Norton. The middle catechism was translated into Greek in 1573. Nowell wrote a still smaller catechism in 1572.

The other catechism mentioned in the Harrow Rules was John Calvin's. He was born in Noyon, France, in 1509, passed most of his life in Geneva, and died in 1564.

TITLE-PAGE AND FIRST PAGE OF THE FIRST BOOK
ON PENMANSHIP IN ENGLISH

WRITING

NEXT, how did Shakespeare learn to write? Foster Watson, in his interesting chapter on writing in the grammar schools, says that writing was regularly taught on the Continent before it was so taught in England, and the first textbook on writing published in England was by a Frenchman. The habit of using professional scriveners may be supposed to have lasted into the sixteenth century, and for a time schools sent their pupils out to them to learn to write, sometimes on holidays, when it was probably optional. Part of this slowness in teaching writing may have been caused by the cost of paper. Paper was not manufactured at all in England till the sixteenth century, and the cost of imported paper was heavy. The *Orders of St. Albans School,* of 1570, which Watson quotes, required each parent to find his child ink, paper, pens, wax candles for winter, and all other things at any time requisite and necessary for the maintenance of his study.

We have already quoted Brinsley's remarks about the average of penmanship in his day. He devotes a whole chapter ("Ludus Literarius", Chap. IV) to the method of teaching writing. Very interesting is his description of the proper way to make a quill pen — and let no casual critic of Shakespeare's writing forget the quill:

> Cause euery one of them to make his own pen; otherwise the making, and mending of pens, will be a very great hinderance, both to the Masters and to the Schollars. Besides that,

when they are away from their Masters (if they haue not a good pen made before) they wil write naught; because they know not how to make their pens themselues.

The best manner of making the pen, is thus:

1. Choose the quil of the best and strongest of the wing, which is somewhat harder, and wil cleaue.

2. Make it cleane, with the backe of the pen-knife.

3. Cleaue it strait vp the backe; first with a cleft, made with your pen-knife: after with another quill put into it, riue it further by little and little, till you see the cleft to be very cleane: so you may make your pen of the best of the quil, & where you see the cleft to be the cleanest, & without teeth. If it doe not cleaue without teeth, cleaue it with your pen-knife in another place, still neerer the backe: for if it be not strait vp the backe, it will very seldome run right. After, make the nebbe and cleft both about one length, somewhat aboue a barley corne breadth, and small; so as it may let downe the inke, and write cleane. Cut the nebbe first slant downewards to make it thinne, and after strait ouerthwart. Make both sides of equall bignesse, vnlesse you bee cunning to cut that side, which lieth vpon the long finger, thinner and shorter; yet so little, as the difference can hardly be discerned. But both of equall length is accounted the surest.

We may presume that the school at Stratford had begun, like the rest, to teach the boys to write. Shakespeare used what was called the "secretary's hand". Now there was

published in London in 1570 the first book on penmanship in the English language. It was by John de Beau Chesne and M. John Baildon, and printed by Thomas Vautrouillier. It is the English version of Beau Chesne's *Le Thrésor de l'Escripture*, printed in Paris in 1550. Beau Chesne was a schoolmaster in Blackfriars. It is probable that the cuts on wood are by Baildon. It was probably in 1570 that Shakespeare entered school, and if we compare the secretary's hand in Beau Chesne with his signature, we find a very close resemblance, especially in his *h's*. Thomas Vautrouillier had as a partner Richard Field, who came from Stratford in 1579. He succeeded Vautrouillier, married his widow, was admitted freeman of the Stationers' Company in 1586, and in 1591 published Shakespeare's *Venus and Adonis*. Beau Chesne's book on penmanship went into a great many editions. The present copy is said to be the only one known of the first English edition. Thirty-seven different styles of writing are given, all with plates. Among them are the bastard secretary, the small bastard secretary, the secretary, the small secretary, the "Secretary written with the lefte hande" (which can be read only with a mirror). The copies are noble and pious sentences, such as these:

> If thou haddest the wisdome of Salomon, the bewtie of Absolon, the puissaunce of Sampson, the long lyfe of Enoch, the richesse of Cresus, the power of Octavian; what can all this auayle the, whan the body is dead.
>
> All men are by nature equal, made all by one workmā of like myre & howesoeuer we deceaue our selues as dere vnto God is the poorest begger as the most pompous Prince liuing in the worlde. Plato.

Shakespeare refers to copy books. See *Loues Labour's lost*, IV (1 F.) [i.e. V], 42: "*Katherine*. Faire as a text B in a Coppie booke."

ROBERT RECORDE

From a recently discovered oil portrait on wood, apparently made from
life, and now in the National Portrait Gallery. The painting bears the
inscription " Robt. Record. M.D. 1556", but this is now so darkened
by age as not to show in the photograph

ARITHMETIC AND GEOMETRY

SHAKESPEARE probably learned his arithmetic from *The Ground of Artes*, by Robert Recorde, Doctor of "Physike". Recorde was born at Tenby, Pembrokeshire, about 1510; he died in Southwark Prison about 1558. He was educated at Oxford and Cambridge, and taught mathematics at Oxford. He became a physician, and wrote on medicine and mathematics.

The edition of *The Ground of Artes* shown on page 73 was printed in 1558. The first edition was probably printed in 1542. It was the first book on arithmetic printed in the English language. If we are to judge from the author's "Verdicte", he had some hesitancy about publishing it.

The Bookes Verdicte

To please or displease sure I am,
But not of one sorte to euery man.
To please the beste sorte woulde I fayne.
The frowarde displease shall I certayne.
Yet wishe I wyll, though not with hope,
All eares and mouthes to please or stoppe.

Notwithstanding the hesitancy of the author the book was used in different editions for more than a hundred and fifty years. It is in the form of question and answer. Its notation is about equally divided between the Arabic and the system of counters, or abacus. In the introduction the student questions the wisdom of studying numbers. The Master says,

If nūbre wer so vile a thing as you dyd esteme it, then nede it not to be vsed so much in mens communication.

71

Exclude noumbre and answere me to this question. How many yeares olde are you?

Scholar. Mum.

M. Howe many daies in a weke? how many wekes in a yeare? What landes hath your father? How many men doth he kepe? Howe longe is it syth you came from hym to me?

Scholar. Mum.

Master. So that if numbre wante, you answere all by Mummes: How many myle to London?

Scholar. A poke full of plummes.

Maister. Why, thus may you see what rule Numbre beareth, and that if numbre be lackyng, it maketh men dombe, so that to moste questions, they must answer Mum.

The same system of dialogue is carried throughout the book, and every example is fully explained by this means. For instance, in the chapter on "Fellowship" the Master says:

Foure men gette a bootye or price in tyme of warre, the prise is in valewe of mony 8190 £, and bicause the men be not of lyke degree, therfore their shares may not be equall, but the chieffest person will haue of the bootye the thyrde parte, and the tenthe parte ouer: the seconde will haue a quarter and the tenthe part ouer; the third will haue the syxt part: and so there is left for the fourth man a verye small portion, but suche is his lot, (whether he be pleased or wroth) he must be content with one XX. parte of the pray. Now I demaunde of you, what shall euery manne haue to his share?

S. You must be fayne to answere to your owne question, els it is not lyke to bee aunswered at this tyme.

The Master then does the problem with full explanation. No opportunity for moral instruction is missed. Thus, in discussing the "Rule of Alligation", the Master says:

Nowe wyll I go in hand with the rule of Alligation, which hath his name, for that by it there are diuers parcels of sundry prices, and sundry quantities allegate, bounde, or myxed togyther, wherby also it might be well called the

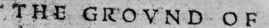

TITLE-PAGE OF RECORDE'S *GROVND OF ARTES*

rule of Myxture, and it hath great use in composition of medicines, and also in myxtures of mettalles, and some vse it hath in myxtures of wines, but I wshe it were lesse vsed therin than it is now a daies. . . . As now by this examples I wil make it playne.

There is IIII. sortes of wyne of seuerall prices, one of 6d a galon, an other of 8d, the thyrde of 11d, and the fourth of 15 pens the galon, of all these wines woulde I haue a mixture made to the summe of 50 gallons, and so that the price of eche galon maye be nine pens. Nowe demaunde I howe muche muste bee taken of euerye sorte of wyne?

Scholar. If it shall please you to worke the first cexample, that I may marke the applyeng of it to the rule, then I truste I shall bee able not onelye to dooe the lyke, but also to se reason in ỹ ordre of the work.

The Master then works the example, and asks the scholar to prove it, which he does satisfactorily. Then the Master gives him a more difficult example, and the scholar works it out with the proof.

There is so much to be learned about social conditions at that time from these examples that one wonders scholars have not used them more!

In those days the counter of a shop was divided by lines into spaces representing units, tens, and hundreds, and counters, sometimes called "reckoning pennies", were used in figuring costs.

In *The Winter's Tale*, IV, iii, the clown says, "I cannot do't without compters."

Recorde published a geometry also, *The pathewaie to knowledge*, which he dedicated to Edward VI, in 1551. Recorde begins his preface to the Gentle Reader thus:

Excuse me, Gentle Reader if ought bee amisse, straunge pathes are not trodé al truly at the first: the way muste needes be comberous, wher none hathe gone before . . . For

74

vnto whiche there are none in the seconde
summe agreeyng, therefore I doo onlye re=
moue those 3 counters from the fyrste sum
into the seconde, as heere dooth appeare.

And so you see
the whole summe
that amounteth of
the Addition of
65436 with 3245,
to be 63681.

And if you haue
marked these two
epsamples well, you
need no farther in=
struction in Addi=

tion of 2 only summes: but if you haue more
then twoo summes to adde , you maye adde
them thus.

Fyrste adde two of them , and then adde
the thyrde and the fourthe or more if there
bee so manny: as if I would adde 2679 with
4286 and 1391. Fyrst I adde the two fyrste
summes thus.

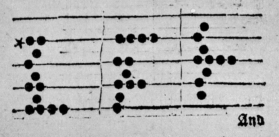

And

neithe is my witte so finely filed, neither my learnyng so largely lettered, neither yet my laisure so quiet and vncombered, that I maie performe iustely so learned a labour, or accordyngly to accomplishe so haultie an enforcemente, yet may I thinke thus : This candle did I light : this light haue I kindeled : . . . I drew the platte rudelie whereon they maye builde, whom God hath indued with learnyng and liuelihod . . .

And this gentle Reader I hartelie protest, where erroure hath happened I wishe it redreste.

There follows a preface to Edward VI, in praise of learning and in defense of geometry, wherein Recorde says :

And before hym [Aristotle] Plato his maister wrote this sentence on his schole house dore, Ἀγεομέτρητος οὐδεὶς εἰσίτω. Let no man entre here (saith he) without knowledge in Geometrie.

In the long preface to the second book Recorde, who seems unable to refrain from riming, bursts into a characteristic bit of bad verse :

Sith Merchauntes by Shippes greate riches doe winne,
   I maie with good right at their feete beginne.
The Shippes on the sea with Saile and with Ore,
   VVere first founde, and still made, by *Geometries* lore.
Their Compas, their Carde, their Pulleis, their Ankers,
   were founde by the skill of wittie *Geometers*.
  .   .   .   .
Yet though other men vnthankfull will be,
   Suruayers haue cause to make muche of me.
And so haue all Lordes, that landes doe possesse :
   But Tenauntes I feare will like me the lesse.
Yet doe I no wrong but measure all truely,
   And yelde the full right to euery man iustely.
Proportion *Geometricall* hath no man opprest,
   If any bee wronged, I wishe it redrest.

Later he informs us that Galen "could neuer cure well a round vlcere, till reason *Geometricall* did teache it hym".

TITLE-PAGE OF RECORDE'S *PATHEWAIE*
TO KNOWLEDGE

He touches on the accusations of necromancy made against geometricians, instancing "Frier Bakon" and adding:

> Great talke there is of a glasse that he made in Oxforde, in whiche men might se thinges that wer doen in other places, and that was iudged to bee doen by power of euill spirites. But I knowe the reason of it to bee good and naturall, and to be wrought by *Geometrie* . . .

There were four books in *The pathewaie*. My copy has but two. The first book has the definitions and conclusions; the second, the "Theoremes", and proofs of the conclusions in the first, for, says Recorde,

> whẽ I haue taught the proposition, as it imported in meanyng, and annexed the demonstration withall, I did perceiue that it was greate trouble, and painfull vexatiõ of mynde to the learner, to comprehende bothe those thynges at ones.

Recorde's definitions are very clear and in language easy for the child to follow.

> Of lines there be twoo principall kindes. The one is called a right, or straight line, and the other a croked line. A straight line is the shortest that maie be drawen betwene twoo prickes.
> And all other lines, that goe not right forthe from pricke to pricke, but boweth any waie, suche are called croked lines.

Recorde's method of interesting his pupils is shown by the last two pages of his first book. He gives the child an informal explanation of how to draw a regular hexagon ("siseangle") inside a given circle, cautioning him to set the foot of the compass "stedily", and giving a good diagram. He then gives three related problems, to make the hexagon outside the circle, and to make the circle inside and outside of it, saying:

> I thought beste to leaue these vnto your owne deuice, that you should studie in some thinges to exercise your wit

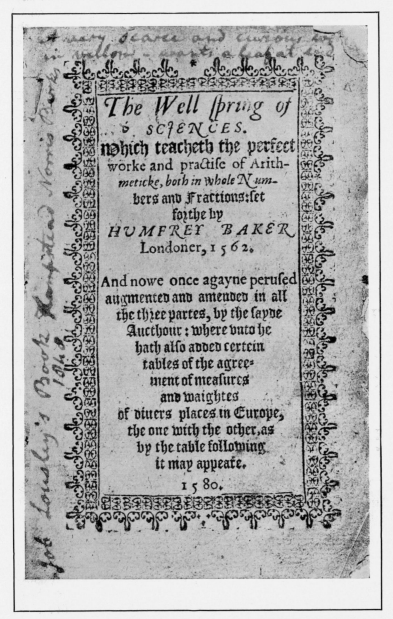

The Well spring of
SCIENCES.
which teacheth the perfect
worke and practise of Arith-
meticke, both in whole Numbers and Fractions: set
forthe by
HVMFREY BAKER
Londoner, 1562.

And nowe once agayne perused
augmented and amended in all
the three partes, by the sayde
Aucthour: where vnto he
hath also added certein
tables of the agree-
ment of measures
and waightes
of diuers places in Europe,
the one with the other, as
by the table following
it may appeare.
1580.

TITLE-PAGE OF BAKER'S *WELL SPRING OF SCIENCES*

> withall . . . . yet this muche I will saie, for your help in woorkyng, that when you shall seeke the centre in a sise-angle (whether it be to make a circle in it either about it) you shall drawe the twoo crosse lines, from one angle to the other angle that lieth against it, and not to the middle of any side, as you did in the cinckangle.

This sort of handling would interest the boy, and make him feel like trying it.

The second dated arithmetic of importance in the English language was Humfrey Baker's *The Well spring of sciences*, 1562. This has no abacus, or system of counters.

Humfrey Baker was born in London. He died about 1580. *The Well spring of sciences* was the only rival to Recorde's arithmetic for many years. The first edition (1562) is not so complete as that of 1580. Baker complains of the criticism of foreigners that English arithmetics are behind those of the Continent. He follows the Continental method, giving the usual operations, — fellowship, barter, alligation, false position, etc.

Another geometry was that of Billingsley, printed in 1570. It has a "Mathematicall Preface" by John Dee, who was evidently much disturbed by having been accused of being adept in the black arts. His comment follows:

> And for these, and such like marueilous Actes and Feates, Naturally, Mathematically, and Mechanically, wrought and contriued: ought any honest Student, and Modest Christian Philosopher, be counted, & called a Coniurer? Shall the folly of Idiotes, and the Mallice of the scornfull, so much preuaile, that He, who seeketh no worldly gaine or glory at their handes: But onely, of God, the threasor of heauenly wisedome, & knowledge of pure veritie: Shall he (I say) in the meane space, be robbed and spoiled of his honest name and fame? . . . For, so, doth the Common

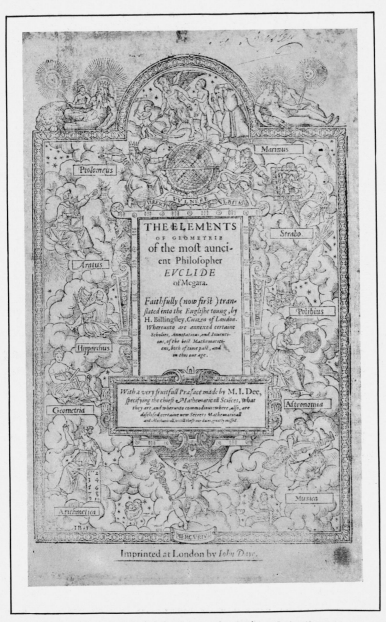

TITLE-PAGE OF BILLINGSLEY'S *ELEMENTS OF GEOMETRIE*

peuish Pratler Imagine and Iangle: And, so, doth the Malicious skorner, secretly wishe, & brauely and boldly face down, behinde my backe. Ah, what a miserable thing, is this kinde of Men? How great is the blindness & boldnes, of the Multitude, in things aboue their Capacitie? . . . O Brainsicke, Rashe, Spitefull, and Disdainfull Countreymen. Why oppresse you me, thus violently, with your slaundering of me: Contrary to Veritie: and contrary to your owne Consciences?

LATIN

WHEN Ben Jonson says that Shakespeare had small Latin and less Greek, he must be read with a knowledge of the fact that what would be "small Latin" in his day was very much more than is mastered by the average American college graduate now. Since boys in country grammar schools were expected to "speak Latin purely and readily", it seems we should seek far today for the few whom Jonson would have regarded as good Latinists.

In any case the first book a boy studied was Lily's Latin Grammar.

William Lily (1468–1522) was appointed headmaster of St. Paul's School by John Colet, the dean. Colet wrote an accidence of the Latin language with rules in English. Lily added the rules of syntax, and Erasmus revised it. The book was called *Absolutissimus de octo orationis partium constructione libellus*, etc.

Foster Watson translates Colet's prefatory letter to the Grammar as follows:

> Methinks, my dear Lily, I bear the same affection to my new school, as a parent to his only son; to whom he is not only willing to pass over his whole estate, but is desirous to impart his own bowels also: and as the father thinks it to little purpose to have begotten a son, unless by diligent education he raises him up into a good and useful man; so to my own mind it is by no means sufficient that I have raised up this school, and have conveyed my whole estate to it, (even during my own life and health), unless I like-

¶ Guillelmi Lilii Angli Rudimenta.

¶ To make latyn

Han I haue an eng: iſſhe to be tourned into latyn/ I ſhall reherſe it twyes/or thryes/ and loke out ẏ verbe.
¶ The verbe.
¶ I may knowe the verbe by ony of theſe wordes: do. dyd. haue. had. wyl ſhal. wold. ſhold. maye. myght. am. art. is. be. was. were can. cowde. let. it. or muſt. whiche ſtade eyther as ſygnes before the verbe/ or elles they be wordes themſelfe. I cal them verbes comenly whan a nowne or pronowne foloweth after them. ¶ If ther̃ come none of this ſygnes in the reaſon/ ẏ worde that anſwered to this queſtẏo/ what do I.thou.or he. what dyd I.thou.or he. ꝛc.ſhall be the
¶ The pryncypall verbe. (verbe.
¶ If there be more verbes than one in ẏ reaſon / the fyrſt is ẏ pryncypall verbe: ſo it be none infinytyue mode/ nor verbe hauynge before hym onyrelatyue/aduerbe/or contiuncc̃on: ẏ cauſeth ẏ reaſon to hange: as.Qui. ẏ whiche Cum:than. Vt: that.
¶ The werbe perſonall.
¶ Whan I knowe my verbe / I muſt loke whether it be perſonall or imperſonall. yf it be perſonall/ it muſt haue a nominatife caſe ioyned w̃ hym expreſſed or vnderſtaded
¶ The nominatyue caſe.
¶ The nominatyue caſe cometh before ẏ verbe/ ꝣ anſwereth to his queſtyon who/ or what: reherſed w̃ the verbe: as. The mayſter loueth his ſcholers. This worde mayſter/ is the nominatyue caſe. for it anſwereth to this queſtyon who loueth.
¶ The nominatyue caſe after the verbe.
Somtyme ẏ noiatyue caſe cometh after ẏ verbe or after ẏ ſygne of ẏ verbe/ as in reaſons Interrogatyues/ optas
A.i.

TITLE-PAGE OF PYNSON'S *GUILLELMI LILII ANGLI
RUDIMENTA*, OF THE FIRST EDITION, c. 1513

wise take all possible care to nurture it in good letters and Christian manners, and bring it on to some useful maturity and perfection. For this reason, master, I send you this small treatise of the Construction of the eight parts of speech (*de constructione octo partium orationis*); small indeed in itself, but such as will afford no small advantage to our scholars, if you will diligently teach and explain it. You know Horace was pleased with brevity in the way of teaching; and I very much approve of his opinion in that matter. If in the reading of the classic authors any notable examples to these rules shall offer themselves it will be your part to mark them as they shall occur. Farewell. From my house. 1513.

If Lily wrote no more of the Grammar than Colet says, it seems strange that the book has always gone by Lily's name. Foster Watson, however, quotes a letter from Erasmus, which explains what happened:

At Colet's command, this book was written by William Lily, a man of no ordinary skill, a wonderful craftsman in the instruction of boys. When he had completed his work, it was handed over to, nay rather thrust upon, me for emendation. What was I to do when the man would not make an end of asking? For he was such a friend that I should think it wrong to deny him any service he might beg of me. Did not a man of such standing deserve of me that by right he should command anything of Erasmus? Accordingly I emended the book by changing many things (for I saw that this was easier for me to do). So that Lily (endowed as he is with too much modesty) did not permit the book to appear with his name, and I (with my sense of candour) did not feel justified that the book should bear my name when it was the work of another. Since both of us refused our names it was published anonymously, Colet merely commending it in a preface. . . . But it seemed good to make these remarks lest afterwards anyone should ascribe to me what I do not claim. There are so many faults to account for in what I have published that no one else ought to

De octo oratio-

NIS PARTIVM CONSTRV-
ctione libellus, cum commen-
tariis Iunii Rabirii.

LVTETIÆ.
Ex officina Ro. Stephani typographi Regii.
M. D. L.

TITLE-PAGE OF THE FIRST FRENCH EDITION OF *DE OCTO
ORATIONIS PARTIVM CONSTRVCTIONE LIBELLVS*

print as mine either what I have not written, or have not even corrected. Farewell, dear reader. Basel. III. Cal. Aug. 1515.

Still other grammarians took a hand in the compilation of this so-called "Lily's Latin Grammar", which, about 1540, was finally authorized by Henry VIII for exclusive use by all "schoolmasters and teachers of grammar within this our realm". During the next two hundred years it was frequently attacked, and a petition was brought against it in the House of Lords in 1758. It was then appropriated as the Eton grammar, and continued up to the time of Doctor Hornby, in 1868.

My early copy of Lily's Latin Grammar was printed by Richard Pynson in 1512 or 1513. The book begins thus:

To make latyn

Whan I haue an englisshe to be tourned into latyn, I shall reherse it twyes or thryes, and loke out $\overset{e}{y}$ verbe.

Another copy of mine is probably the syntax (by Lily) of the large compilation described above. It is a variation of the *Absolutissimus de octo orationis partium constructione libellus*, etc., mentioned above, and contains the letter of Colet to Lily that we have quoted ("haud aliter mihi uideor affectus in nouam hanc scholam nostram, Lili charissime, quam in unicum filium pater"). Printed in Paris by Stephanus in 1550, it is in Latin and French. The commentaries are by Junius Rabirius.

Colet's whole theory of the teaching of grammar is given at the end of his "Introduction to the Accidence". I quote this from Foster Watson, who has modernized the spelling:

Let the pupil above all busily learn and read good Latin authors of chosen poets and orators, and note wisely how

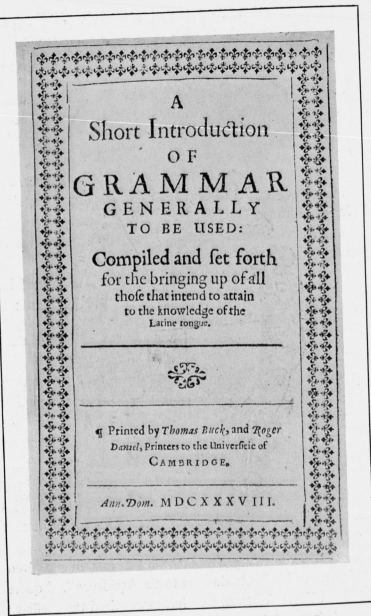

A
Short Introduction
OF
GRAMMAR
GENERALLY
TO BE USED:

Compiled and set forth
for the bringing up of all
those that intend to attain
to the knowledge of the
Latine tongue.

¶ Printed by *Thomas Buck*, and *Roger
Daniel*, Printers to the University of
CAMBRIDGE.

Ann. Dom. MDCXXXVIII.

TITLE-PAGE OF LILY'S LATIN GRAMMAR

5ᵐ Imitativa.

A primo
casu in t.

Imitativa sunt, quæ imitationem significant : ut, Patrisso, Atticisso, Platonisso. At Latini hâc formâ non adeò delectati sunt : unde pro Græcisso, Græcor usi sunt : ut, Cornicor, à cornice; vulpinor, à vulpe; Bacchor, à Baccho.

DE PERSONA.

Tres sunt verbi personæ : Prima, ut Lego; Secunda, ut Legis; Tertia, ut Legit.

DE NUMERO.

Numeri sunt duo : Singularis, ut Lego; Pluralis, ut Legimus.

DE CONJUGATIONE.

Quandoquidem de conjugandorum verborum ratione in rudimentis Anglicis traditum est, quæ pueri tanquam ungues suos exactissimè callere debent:proximum fuerit, ut hæ Guliel. Lilii de præteritis & supinis regulæ (lucidissimæ quidem illæ compendiosissimæq;, nec sanè minùs utiles) pari aviditate imbibantur.

G. LIL. DE SIMPLICIUM
verborum primæ Conjugatio-
nis communi Præterito.

As, avi.

*Hyperme-
ter versus
plus justo
unâ syllabâ
constat, sed
collidenda
cum prima
voce se-
quentis
versûs; id
quod om-
nium com-
mune est.

AS in præsenti perfectum format in
avi ;

Ut, no, nas, navi: vocito, vocitas, vo-
citavi :

Deme lavo, lavi: juvo, juvi; nexóque,
nexui ; *

Et seco, quod secui: neco, quod necui; micó verbum
Quod micui, plico quod plicui, frico quod fricui datt
Sic domo quod domui, tono quod tonui, sono verbum
Quod sonui, crepo quod crepui, veto quod vetui dat,
Atque cubo, cubui : raró hæc formantur in avi.
Do, das, ritè dedi; sto, stas, formare steti vult.

Secun-

they wrote and spoke, and study alway to follow them; desiring none other rules but their examples. For in the beginning men spoke not Latin because such rules were made but contrariwise because men spoke such Latin upon that followed the rules and (so) were made. That is to say, Latin speech was before the rules, not the rules before the Latin speech.

That only authors are to be taught convenient and most to purpose unto the true Latin speech. All barbary, all corruption, all Latin adulteration which ignorant, blind fools brought into the world and with the same hath disdained and poisoned the old Latin speech of the early Roman tongue will not be allowed entrance to the school.

I say that filthiness and all such abusion which the later world brought in, which more rather may be called blotheration than literature I utterly abbanish and exclude out of this school.

H. R. D. Anders, in *Shakespeare's Books*, gives many quotations from Shakespeare whence the inference may justly be drawn that Lily's Latin Grammar was the one Shakespeare studied. The following (quoted from Anders) is a case in point:

In *Titus Andronicus*, IV, we find Horace quoted:

> Integer vitæ scelerisque purus,
> Non eget maury iaculis nec arcus.

Chiron, on hearing the lines, observes, "O, 'tis a verse in *Horace*. I know it well. I read it in the Grammer long agoe." The couplet stands twice in Lily's Grammar: on leaf 23 as an instance of the ablative case . . .

After Lily's Latin Grammar, Shakespeare would ordinarily have studied *Sententiae pueriles*. This begins with a page of aphorisms two words long; then follow sentences in three words, then in four; then in more. There are also pious sentences to be studied on holy days.

90

※※※※※※※※※※※※※※※※※

Sentences (or Sayings) of wife Men, colleſted for them that firſt enter to the Latin Tongue.

Sapientum Sententiæ præprimis Latinæ Linguæ Tyronibus, Colleſtæ.

Sentences of two Words. *Sententiæ duarum Diſtionum.*

HELP thy Friends.
　Abſtain from other
Conceal a ſecret (mens things
Be eaſy to be ſpoken to.
5 Try thy Friends.
Fool-hardineſs is dangerous.
Make uſe of thy Friends
　Honour good men.
Be kind ſpoken.
10 Do well to good men
Say well to all men
　Know thy ſelfe.
Reſpeſt thy kinsfolk.
Follow concord.
15 Hate ſlandering.
Adviſe blameleſly.
　Fear couzenage.
Keep a thing given.
Reſtore a thing depoſited.
20 Accuſe no man.
Delight thy friends.
Uſe Diligence.
　Keep thy credit. (mad.
Drunkenneſs makes men
25 Shun Drunkenneſs.

A Micis opitulare.
　Alienis abſtine.
Arcanum cela.
Affabilis eſto.
5 Amicos probato.
Audacia periculoſa.
Amicis utere.
　Bonos honora.
Blandus eſto.
10 Bonis benefacito.
Benedic omnibus.
　Cognoſce teipſum.
Cognatos cole.
Concordiam ſeſtare.
15 Calumniam oderis.
Conſule inculpate.
　Dolum time.
Datum ſerva.
Depoſitum redde.
20 Deſerto neminem.
Deleſta amicos.
Diligentiam adhibe.
Exiſtimationem retine.
Ebrietas dementat.
25 Ebrietatem ſuge.

A 2　　　　　　　　Exerciſe

A PAGE FROM HOOLE'S *SENTENTIAE*

CATONIS

DISTICHA MORA=
lia ex caſtigatione D. Eraſmi
Roterodami vna cum annotationibus
et ſcholijs Rechardi Tauerneri An=
glico idiomata conſcriptis
in vſum Anglicæ
iuuentis.

Aliquot ſentenciæ in ſignes
ex variis collectæ ſcriptoribus
per eundem Eraſmum.

Mimi publiani, cũ Anglicis
eiuſdem Rechardi ſcholiis, re=
cogniti.

LONDINI
ex edibus Nicolai Montani.
Anno ſalutis.

1553.

TITLE-PAGE OF CATO'S *DISTICHA MORALIA*

Cato's *Disticha* often follows the *Sententiae pueriles*

After learning many of these sentences, the child advanced to Cato's *Disticha moralia* or the *Flores aliquot sententiarum*.

Next would come Corderius's *Dialogues*. Maturinus Corderius, born in Normandy in 1479, was the teacher of John Calvin at the Collège de la Marche. Corderius wrote his *Dialogues* in 1564, when he was eighty-five years old. This was a great textbook, and it went through many different editions in other languages. It consisted of a series of lively dialogues, of which I quote but one.

COLLOQUY LXVIII

A. Adfuistíne *concione sacræ* hodie?

Were you present *at the sermon* to day?

B. Adfui.

I was present.

A. Quis *habuit concionem?*

Who *preached the Sermon?*

B. Dominus N——

Mr. N——.

A. Quotâ horâ *incepit?*

At what Hour *did he begin?*

B. Septimâ.

At the Seventh.

A. Unde *sumpsit* thema?

Whence *took he* his Text?

B. Ex Epistolâ *Pauli* ad Romanos.

Out of the Epistle *of Paul* to the Romans.

A. Quoto capite?

What Chapter?

B. Octavo.

The Eighth.

A. Respondisti *adhuc* bene: *nunc* videamùs *quid* sequatur? *Ecquid mandâsti* memoriæ?

You have answered *yet* well: *now* let us see *what* may follow: *Have you committed any Thing to Memory?*

B. Nihil *quod* possum *referre.*

Nothing *that* I can *say.*

A. Nihil! *cogita* paulisper, *et* vide *ne turberis* quin *esto* bono animo.

Nothing! *think* a little, *and* see *you be not disturbed*, but *be* of good Courage.

B. Certè *possum* reminisci *nihil.*

Indeed I *can* remember *nothing.*

A. Ne verbum quidem?

Not so much as a Word?

B. Nihil prorsus.

Nothing at all.

A. Hem *verbero!* Quid *profecisti* igitur?

Ho *you Rogue!* what *have you profited* then?

B. Nescio, *nisi* quòd *abstinui* fortasse *interim* à malis.

I know not, *but* that *I have abstained* perhaps *in the mean time* from evil Things.

PRINCIPIA LA-
TINE LOQVENDI,
SCRIBENDIQVE
SIVE,

Selecta quædam ex Ciceronis epistolis, ad
pueros in Latina lingua exercendos, adiecta interpretatione Anglica, & (vbi
opus esse visum est) Latina declaratio-
ne. Ad rationem quam nuper suis sedu-
litate summa Gallicè conscripsit.

Maturinus Corderius.

*A very necessary and profitable en-
traunce to the speakyng and wri-
tyng of the Latin tongue.*
Or
A certain draught taken out of Ciceroes Epistles, for the exercise of children in the Latin
speache together with an easy and a familiar
construction thereof into Englishe.

¶Opusculum ad conuertendam Latini sermonis
puritatem in nostri vernaculi vsum & fami-
liaritatem literario tyrocinio apprimè
accomodum, gratum, iuxtà ac vtile.

Translated by T. W.

Anno dñi. 1575.

TITLE-PAGE OF CORDERIUS

A. Istud, *quidem*, est *aliquid* si *potuit* fieri, *ut* abstinueris *à malo* omnino.

That, *indeed*, is *something*, if *it could* be, *that* you shall abstain *from Evil* altogether.

B. Abstinui *quoad* potui.

I have abstained *as much as* I could.

A. Fac *esse* ita, *tamen* non satisfecistî *Deo*, quum *scriptum sit*, declina *à malo* et *fac* bonum; *sed* dic *mihi* quaeso, *quâ gratiâ* ivisti *illùc* potissimum.

Suppose *it to be* so, *yet* you have not satisfied *God*, seeing *it is written*, fly *from Evil* and *do* Good; *but tell me*, I pray, *on what Account* went you *there* chiefly?

B. Ut *addiscerem* aliquid.

That *I might learn* something.

A. Cur *non fecisti istud?*

Why *did you not do that?*

B. Non potui.

I could not.

A. Non potuisti, *nebulo!* imò *noluisti*, aut *certè* non curâsti.

You could not, *you Rogue!* nay, *you would not*, or *certainly* you did not care.

B. Cogor *fateri.*

I am forced *to confess.*

A. Quae res *cogit* te?

What thing *forceth* you?

B. Mea conscientia, quae accusat *me* apud Deum.

My Conscience, *which* accuseth *me* to God.

A. Dicis *rectè*, utinam *ex animo.*

You say *right*, I wish *from your Mind.*

B. Equidem *dico* ex animo.

Truly *I speak* from my Mind.

A. Potest *fieri* ita, *sed* age, *quae* fuit *causa* quamobrem *mandaveris* nihil *memoriæ?*

It may *be* so, *but* come, *what* was *the Reason* why *you* committed nothing *to Memory?*

B. Mea *negligentia*; nam *non audiebam* diligenter.

My *Negligence*, for *I did not hear* diligently.

A. Quid *faciebas* igitur?

What *did you do* then?

B. Identidem *dormiebam.*

Now and then *I slept.*

A. Ita *soles*; sed *quid* agebas *in reliquo tempore?*

So *you use*; but *what* did you do *in the rest of the Time?*

B. Cogitabam *mille* ineptias, *ut* pueri *solent.*

I thought of *a thousand* Fooleries, *as* Boys *are wont.*

A. An tu es *adeò puer* ut *non debeas* esse *attentus* ad audiendum *verbum* Dei?

Are you *so much a Child* that *you ought not* to be *attentive* to hear *the Word* of God?

B. Si *essem* attentus, *possem* proficere *aliquid.*

If *I were* attentive, *I might* profit *something.*

A. Quid *igitur* meruisti?

What *then* have you deserved?

B. Verbera.

Stripes.

A. Meruisti *profectò*, idque *largissimè.*

You have deserved *indeed*, and that *very plentifully.*

B. Confiteor *ingenuè.*

I confess *ingenuously.*

95

A. Para *te* ad recipiendas *plagas*.

B. Ah! *magister*, ignosce *obsecro*, peccavi, *fateor*, sed *ex nullâ malitiâ*.

A. Quid *facies* igitur *si* ignovero *tibi?*

B. Faciem *meum* officium *posthac* ut *spero*.

A. Addendum erat, *Deo* juvante.

B. Imò, *magister*, praestabo *meum* officium *posthac* Deo *juvante*.

A. Age, *condono* hanc culpam *tuis lacrymis*, et *ignosco* tibi *eâ lege* ut *memineris* tui promissi.

B. Ago *tibi* gratias, *humanissime* praeceptor.

A. Eris in *maximâ gratiâ* apud me, *si* servaveris *promissa*.

Make ready *yourself* to receive *Stripes*.

Ah! *Master*, pardon me *I pray you*, I have done amiss, *I confess*, but *from no ill Purpose*.

What *will you do* then, *if* I shall pardon *you?*

I will do *my* duty *hereafter*, as *I hope*.

You should have added, *God* helping.

Yes, *Master*, I will perform *my* Duty *hereafter*, God *helping*.

Well, *I forgive* this Fault *to your Tears*, and *I pardon* you *upon this Condition*, that *you be mindful* of your Promise.

I give *you* Thanks, *most humane* Master.

You will be *in very great Favour* with me, *if* you will keep your *Promise*.

Erasmus (1466–1536) made, in 1499, his first trip to England, where he was associated with Colet, More, Linacre, and Grocyn. His *Colloquies* are as dramatic as those of Corderius, but perhaps not so interesting to small boys. As a sample of their quality we quote a few lines from an American edition, by Isaiah Thomas, Jr., published at Worcester, Massachusetts, in 1801.

THE SHIPWRECK

B. Autem *in primis*, inquit, navis est *exoneranda*, sic *necessitas* jubet *durum* telum: *Præstat* consulere *vitae*, dispendio *rerum* quam *interire* simul *cum* rebus. *Veritas* persuasit: *plurima* vasa *plena* preciosis *mercibus* projecta sunt *in mare*.

But *first*, quoth he, *the ship is to be unloaded*; so *necessity* commands, *a hard* weapon: *It is better* to take care *of life*, with the loss *of goods*, than to *perish* together *with our goods*. *Truth* persuaded; *very many* vessels *full* of precious *wares* were thrown *into the sea*.

96

TITLE-PAGE OF ERASMUS'S *COLLOQVIES*

ERASMUS

Property of the author

A. Hoc *erat* vere *facere* jacturam.

B. Quidam *Italus* aderat, *qui* egerat legatum *apud regem Scotiae*, huic erat *scrinium* plenum *argenteis* vasis, *annulis* panno, *et* sericis *vestimentis*.

A. Nolebat *is* decidere *cum* mari?

B. Non, *sed* cupiebat *aut* perire *cum* suis *amicis* opibus, *aut* servari *simul* cum *illis*; itaque *refragabat*.

A. Quid *dixit* nauclerus?

B. Liceret tibi *per nos*, inquit *ille*, perire *solum* cum *tuis*; sed *non æquum est*, ut *nos* omnes *periclitemur* causa *tui* scrinii *alioqui* dabimus *te* praecipitem *in mare* una *cum* scrinio.

A. Orationem *vere* nauticam!

B. Sic *Italus* quoque *fecit* jacturam, *precans* multa *mala* superis et inferis, *quod* credidisset *suam* vitam *tam barbaro* elemento; *paulo* post *venti* facti *nihilo* mitiores *nostris* muneribus, rupere funes, *disjecere* vela.

. . . .

A. Quid *interea* vectores?

B. Ibi *vidisses* miseram *faciem* rerum. *Nautæ*, canentes *salve* regina, *implorabant* virginem *matrem*, appellantes *eam* stellam *maris*, reginam *cœli*, dominam *mundi*, portam *salutis*, ac *blandientes* illi *multis* aliis *titulis*, quos *sacræ* literæ nusquam *tribuunt* illi.

A. Quid illa cum mari, quae nunquam navigavit, opinor?

This *was* truly *to make loss*.

A certain *Italian* was there, *who* had been ambassador *with* the king *of Scotland*, he had *a box* full *of silver* vessels, *rings*, cloth *and* silk *clothes*.

Would not *he* compound *with* the sea?

No, *but* he desired *either* to perish *with* his *beloved* riches, *or* to be saved *together* with *them*; *therefore he refused*.

What *said* the master?

You might, *for us*, quoth *he*, perish *alone* with *your things*; but *it is not fit* that *we* all *should be endangered* for the sake of *your* box, *otherwise* we will throw *you* headlong *into the sea*, together *with* your box.

A speech *truly* sailor like!

So *the Italian* too *made* loss; *wishing* many *evil things* to these above *and* below, *that* he had trusted *his* life to *so barbarous* an element: *A little* after, *the winds*, made *nothing* milder *by our* presents, *broke* the ropes, *tore away* the sails.

. . . .

What *in the mean time did* the passengers?

There *you would have seen* a miserable *face* of things. *The sailors*, singing, *God save you*, O queen, *implored* the virgin *mother*, calling *her* the star *of the sea*, the queen *of heaven*, lady *of the world*, harbor *of safety*, and *flattering* her *with many* other *titles*, which *the holy* scriptures *no where* attribute *to her*.

What has she to do *with* the sea, *who* never *sailed*, I believe?

B. Venus *olim* agebat *curam* nautarum, *quia* credebatur *nata* ex mari; *quoniam* ea *desivit* curare, *virgo* mater *est* suffecta *huic* matri, *non* virgini.

Venus *formerly* took *care* of the sailors, *because* she was believed to be *born* of the sea; *because* she *has ceased* to take care, the *virgin* mother *is* substituted *to this* mother, *not* a virgin.

A. Ludis.

You banter.

B. Nonnulli *procumbentes* in *tabulas* adorabant *mare*, effundentes *quicquid* olei *erat* in undas, *blandientes* illi *non* aliter *quam* solemus *irato* principi.

Some *falling down* upon *the boards*, worshipped *the sea*, pouring *whatsoever* oil *there was* into the waves, *flattering* it *no* otherwise *than* we use to do *an angry* prince.

A. Quid *aiebant?*

What *did they say?*

B. O clementissimum *mare!* O generosissimum *mare!* O formosissimum *mare!* mitesce, *serva.* Occinebant *multa* hujuscemodi *surdo* mari.

O most merciful *sea!* O most noble *sea!* O most rich *sea!* grow mild, *save us.* They sung *many things* of this kind *to the deaf sea.*

A. Ridicula *superstitio!* Quid *alii?*

Ridiculous *superstition!* What did *others?*

B. Quidam *nihil* aliud *quam* vomebant, *plerique* nuncupabant *vota.* Aderat *quidam* Anglus, *qui* promittebat *aureos* montes *virgini* Walsingamicae, *si* attigisset *terram* vivus. *Alii* promittebant *multa* ligno *crucis* quod *esset* in *tali* loco, *alii* rursus quod *esset* in *tali* loco. Idem *factum est* de *virgine* Maria *quae* regnat *in* multis *locis* et *putant* votum *irritum*, nisi *exprimas* locum.

Some did *nothing* else *than* vomit, *most* put up *vows.* There was there *a certain* Englishman *who* promised *golden* mountains *to the maid* of Walsingham, if he touched *land* alive. *Others* promised *many things* to the wood of the *cross*, which *was* in *such* a place, *others* again to that *which* was *in* such *a place.* The same *was done* as to *the virgin* Mary, *who* reigns *in* many *places*, and *they think* the vow *to no purpose*, unless *you express* the place.

. . . .

A. Nemo *meminit* Christophori?

. . . .

Did nobody *mention* Christopher?

B. Audivi *unum* non *sine* risu, *qui* clara *voce*, ne *non exaudiretur*, polliceretur *Christophoro*, qui *est* Lutetiæ *in summo templo*, mons *verius* quam *statua*, cereum *tantum* quantus *esset ipse.* Cum *vociferans* hæc *quantum* poterat,

I heard *one*, not *without* smiling, *who* with a clear *voice*, lest *he should not be heard* promised *Christopher*, who *is* at Paris, *on the top of a church*, a mountain *more truly* than *a statue*, a wax candle *as big as he was himself.*

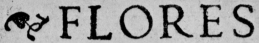

FLORES

ALIQVOT SENTEN=
TIARVM EX VARIIS
collecti scriptoribus.

❦THE FLOWERS OF SEN
cies gathered out of sundry wry=
ters by Erasmus in Latine
& Englished by Richard
Tauerner.

❦ Huic libello non male conueniẽt
Mimi illi Publiani nuper ab eo=
dem Richardo versi.

❦LONDINI.
Ex aedibus Wilhelmi Middiltoñ
Anno.M.D.XLVII.

TITLE-PAGE OF THE *FLORES ALIQVOT SENTENTIARVM*

This book also was used in the instruction in Latin

inculcaret identidem; *qui* forte *astabat* proximus, *notus* illi, *tetigit* eum *cubito*, ac *submonuit*, Vide *quid* pollicearis, *etiam si* facias *auctionem* omnium tuarum *rerum*, non fueris solvendus. *Tum* ille *inquit* voce *jam* pressiore, *videlicit*, ne *Christophorus* exaudiret, *Tace*, fatue; *an credis* me *loqui* ex animo? *Si* semel *contigero* terram, *non daturus sum* ei *sebaceam* candelam.

A. O crassum *ingenium!* suspicio *fuisse* Batavum.

B. Non *sed* erat *Zelandus*.

A. Miror *Paulum* Apostolum *venisse* nulli in mentem, *qui* navigavit *ipse* olim, et nave *fracta*, desilierit *in terram*, nam *is* haud ignarus *mali* didicit *succurrere* miseris.

B. Erat *nulla* mentio *Pauli*.

A. Precabantur *interim?*

B. Certatim. *Alius* canebat, *salve* regina; *alius*, credo, *in Deum*. Erant *qui* habebant *quasdem* peculiares *preculas*, non *dissimiles* magicis, *adversus* pericula.

A. Ut *religiosos* afflictio *facit!* Secundis rebus, nec Deus *nec* divus *venit* in mentem: *Quid* tu *interea?* nuncupabas *vota* nulli *divorum?*

B. Nequaquam.

A. Cur *ita?*

When *bawling out* this *as hard as* he could, *he inculcated it* now and then; *he that* by chance *stood* next, *known* to him, *touched* him *with his elbow*, and *advised him*, have a care *what* you promise, *for though* you make *an auction* of all your *goods*, you will not be able to pay. *Then* he *says* with a voice, *now* lower, *to wit*, lest *Christopher* should hear, *hold your tongue*, you fool; *do you think* I *speak* from my heart? *if* once *I touch* land, *I will* not give him *a tallow* candle.

O gross *wit!* I suspect *he was* a Dutchman.

No, *but he* was a *Zealander*.

I wonder *that Paul* the Apostle *came* into nobody's mind, *who* sailed *himself* formerly, *and* the ship *being wrecked*, leaped out *upon land*; for *he* not being ignorant *of evil* has learnt *to succor* the miserable.

There was *no* mention *of Paul*.

Did they pray *in the mean time?*

Hard. *One* sung, *God save you* O queen; *another*, I believe *in God*. There were *who had some* peculiar *prayers*, not *unlike* magical ones, *against* dangers.

How *religious* affliction *makes us!* in prosperity, *neither* God *nor* saint *comes* into our mind: *What* did you *in the mean time?* did you make *vows* to none *of the saints?*

Not at all.

Why *so?*

An early book used in Latin and in Greek was Æsop's Fables. Hoole says Æsop's Fables are to be turned from Greek into English, then from English into Latin, and from the Latin back into Greek in the fifth form.

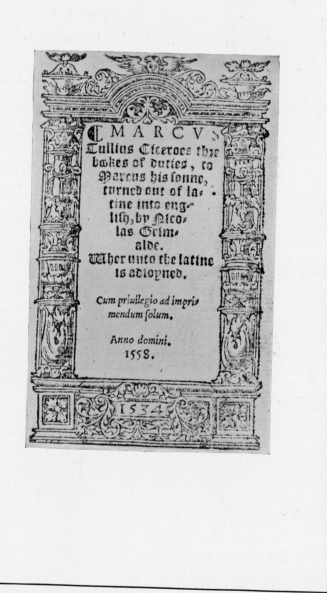

TITLE-PAGE OF CICERO'S *BOOKES OF DVTIES*

This volume was widely used to illustrate the teaching of manners and conduct

I have several Æsops, among them a nicely illustrated one printed in London in 1551, which has the Greek in the left-hand column, and Latin in the right.

Anders gives many allusions to Æsop from Shakespeare. I quote five out of fifteen.

> Gloucester's hint, 3. Henry VI., Act V, v, 23, that the masculine queen, Margaret, should have always "worn the petticoat, And ne'er have stol'n the breech from Lancaster", is met by the young Prince with the following caustic retort, containing an allusion to Gloucester's figure crooked like that of Æsop:
>
>> Let *Æsop fable* in a winter's night;
>> His currish riddles sort not with this place.

Strange to say, Henry Green infers from this passage that Shakespeare had a low estimate of Æsop's fables. But the expression "His currish (malicious) riddles" in no wise warrants this inference. The words must be taken *cum grano salis* as referring to what Gloucester had just remarked, and not as derogatory from Æsop. The apt illustrations which Shakespeare drew from the famous fables leave no doubt that the poet had no mean opinion of them.

1. *The fable of the Countryman and a Snake* is alluded to in 2. Henry VI., Act III, i, 343:

> I fear me you but warm the starved snake,
> Who, cherish'd in your breasts, will sting your hearts.

Compare, too, Richard II., Act III, ii, 129–131:

> *K. Rich.* O villains, vipers, damn'd without redemption! . . .
> Snakes, in my heart-blood warm'd that sting my heart!

And Act V, iii, 57:

> Forget to pity him, lest thy pity prove
> A serpent that will sting thee to the heart.

2. *The Crow and the Borrowed Feathers* is alluded to by Shakespeare (who, by the way, was himself once called 'an upstart crow, beautified with our feathers', by the dying Greene) in 2. Henry VI., Act III, i, 69 ff.

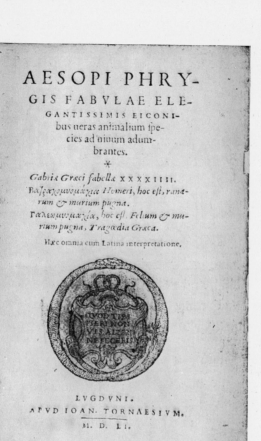

TITLE-PAGE OF *AESOPI FABVLAE*

Æsop's Fables was another widely used textbook for the teaching of morals

King . . . Our Kinsman Gloucester is as innocent
From meaning treason to our royal person
As is the sucking lamb or harmless dove . . .
Queen . . . Seems he a dove? *his feathers are but borrow'd.*
For he's disposed as the hateful raven:
Is he a lamb? etc. (cf. below.)

Another popular book was the *Bucolica* of Battista Span-
uoli, called Mantuanus. "Which is a poet both for style and
matter very familiar and grateful to children, and therefore
read in most schools". (Hoole.) Mantuanus was "born in
1448 and died in 1516. He was a Carmelite for many years
but retiring in 1513, gave himself up to the *belles-lettres*
entirely. The Duke of Mantua erected to his memory a
marble statue crowned with laurel, and placed it next to
that of Vergil, and even Erasmus went so far as to say that
a time would come when Baptist Mantuan would not be
placed much below his illustrious countryman". (Foster
Watson)

The possibility that Shakespeare studied the *Bucolica* is
suggested by Holofernes' speech in *Loues Labour's lost*,
Act IV (1 F) [i.e. V], wherein he quotes from the first
eclogue

*Facile precor gellida, quando pecas omnia sub vmbra
ruminat,* and so forth. Oh, good old *Mantuan,* I may
speake of thee as the traueiler doth of *Venice, vemchie,
vencha, que non te vnde, que non te perreche.* Old *Mantuan,*
old *Mantuan.* Who vnderstandeth thee not. . . .

It is also possible that Shakespeare, like many other little
boys, never got beyond the first eclogue.

In the edition of 1504 the editor gives three or four lines
of the eclogue, then as commentary a page or more of notes
(in Latin), then a few lines more followed by notes, and so

θὲὶς τοῖς ἀνέμοις , ῥᾳ-
δίως δὶεσώθη. ἡ δ᾽ ἐ-
λαία ἐπειδὴ ἀντίτεινε
τοῖς ἀνέμοις , κατεκλά-
σθη τῆ βίᾳ.

Ἐπιμύθιον.

Ὁ μῦθ Ο δηλοῖ, ὅτι
οἱ τῶ καιρῶ κὴ τοῖς κρείτ
τοσιν αὐτῶν μὴ ἀνδι-
σάμθμοι, κρείττες ἐσι τ
πρὸς μείζονας φιλονει-
κούντων.

nata ventis , facilè
euasit , oliua au-
tem cùm ventis re-
stitisset , vi diffra-
cta est.

AFFABVLATIO.

Fabula significat.
eos qui tempori ac præ-
stantioribus non resi-
stunt , meliores esse ijs
qui cum potentioribus
contendunt.

Λύκ Ο κỳ Γέ-
ρανΟ.

LVPVS ET
Grus. 144

Λύκου λαιμῶ ἰ-
σίον ἐπεπήγει. ὁ
ἢ Γεράνῳ μισθον πα-
ρέξειν

Vp⁹ gutturi os-
se infixo , mer-
cedem Grui se præbi-
s turum

on, all in the same type on the same page, so that the child gets the full meaning of the poem without the effort of turning to notes in the back.

Ocland's *Anglorum Prælia* contains a poetic history of English battles on land and sea from Edward III to Queen Mary, and then of the peaceful, prosperous government of Queen Elizabeth from her accession to 1582. There follows a prose narrative, by Alexander Neville, of William Kett's insurrection. The work was appointed by Queen Elizabeth and her Privy Council to be received and taught in every grammar and free school within the kingdom "for the remouing of such lasciuious poets as are commonly reade and taught in the said grammar schooles".

The Tenour of the Letters

Directed by the Lords of hir highnesse priuie Counsell to hir Maiesties high cōmissioners in causes Ecclesiasticall, for the publike receyuing and teaching of Ch. Ocklandes Booke in all Grammer & freescholes within this Realme.

After our right harty commendations Whereas there hath beene of late, a booke written in Latin verse by one *Christopher Ockland,* intituled *Anglorum Praelia,* about halfe a yeare sithence imprinted and published, and nowe againe lately reprinted with the addition of a short treatise or appendix concerning the peaceable gouernement of the Queenes Maieftie; Forasmuch as his trauell therein, with the qualitie of the Werke, hath received good commendation, and that the subject or matter of the saide booke, is such, as is worthy to bee reade of al men&, especially in common scholes, where diuers heathen Poets are ordinarily reade and taught, from the which the youth of the realme doth rather receiue infection in maners, than aduancement in vertue : in place of some of which Poets, we thinke this booke fitte to bee reade and taught in the Grāmer Schooles : We haue therefore thought good, as well for the encouraging

F. Baptiste Mantuani

Bucolica seu adolescentia in decem æglogas
diuisa. Ab Iodoco Badio Ascensio familiari
ter exposita: cum indice dictionum.

Carmen eiusdem de sancto Iohanne Baptista

Dialogus eiusdem de vita beata.

¶ In Aeglogas Mantuani Decatosticon
omnium earum argumenta cõplectens:
Ioannis Gallinarij Budorini.

Perlege Mantoi ruralia carmina vatis
Perlege pastoreos lector amice iocos
Non hic lascinum Coridonis laudat Alexim̄
Pagina nocturnos nec docet ista dolos
Fœmineas artes fastus conuicia fraudes
Exprobrat:& paphiæ furta facesᵭ deæ
Q̃ tenuis sanctæ sit honos & cura poæsis
Et scurras gratos regibus esse dolet
Increpat urbanos vario discrimine mores:
Cætera de sacra relligione canunt.

TITLE-PAGE OF THE *BVCOLICA* OF MANTUANUS

of the saide *Ocklande* and others, that are learned, to
bestow their trauel and studies to so good purposes, as also
for the benefite of the youth and the remouing of such
lasciuious Poets as are commonly read and taught in the
saide scholes (the matter of this booke being heroical and
of good instruction) to pray and require you upon the sight
hereof, as by our speciall order, to write your Letters unto
all the Bishoppes thorough out this Realme, requiring them
to give commandement, that in all the Grammer and freescholes with in their seueral Dioceses, the saide Bookes,
de Anglorum Praeliis, and peaceable gouernement of hir
maiestie, may bee in place of some of the heathen Poets,
receiued and publyquely read and taught by the Schoolemasters unto theyr Scholers in some one fourme in their
Schole, fittest for that matter. Whereof praying you there
may be no defaulte, so as this our direction may take place
accordingly, Wee bid you hartily farewel : from the Court
at Greenewich, the 21, of Aprill. 1582.

Your Louing Friendes

EDWARD LINCOLNE, ROBERT LEICESTER, AMBROSE
WARWICK, FRANCIS KNOLLYS, JAMES CROFTS,
CHRISTOPHER HATTON, FRANCIS WALSINGHAM.

One more method of improving the pupil's Latin was by
debates.

The Harrow Statutes of 1580 required the schoolmaster
every day for an hour "to hear either the third, fourth or
fifth forms amongst themselves propound questions and
answers one to another of cases, declinings, comparison of
nouns, etc. . . . . so that every of these forms shall every
week use this exercise twice, and they which answer the
first time shall propound question the latter time, and they
which do best shall go, sit and have place before their fellows
for the time".

Disputations were common in the schools of England
when Shakespeare was a student. One of the best books on

ANGLORVM PRÆLIA

ab anno Domini.1327.anno
nimirùm primo inclytiſsimi Princi-
pis Eduardi eius nominis tertij,vſque ad annū
Domini.1558.Carmine ſummatim perſtriƈta.

ITEM.

De pacatiſſimo Angliæ ſtatu, imperante Eliza-
betha,compendioſa Narratio.

Authore CHRISTOPHORO OCLANDO, primò
Scholæ Southwarkienſis propè Londinum,dein
Cheltennamenſis,quæ ſunt à ſereniſsima ſua
Maieſtate fundatæ,Moderatore.

Hæc duo Poëmata, iam ob argumenti grauitatem
quàm Carminis facilitatem, Nobiliſſimi Regiæ Maieſtatis
Conſiliarij in omnibus huius regni Scholis præ-
legenda pueris præſcripſ unt.

Hijs Alexandri Neuilli K E T T V M : tùm propter argumenti ſimilitudinem,tùm propter orationis
elegantiam adiunximus.

LONDINI:

Apud Radulphum Nuberie,ex aſſignatione
Henrici Bynneman Typographi.A N N O.1582.

Cum priuilegio Regiæ Maieſtatis.

TITLE-PAGE OF OCLAND'S *ANGLORVM PRÆLIA* (1582)

the subject was that of John Stockwood. The subjects for debate were drawn from grammar. This was a survival of the old method of dialectics transferred to the study of grammar, the object being to sharpen the boy's wits and teach him to maintain an argument on any subject.

SECOND DISPUTATION

[Second Question]

Whether five declensions of nouns are sufficient, so that there is no noun which cannot be included in some one of them. And whether the grammatical rules which are handed down concerning these are true.

QUESTOR. My ability is not such that I can soothe your ears with a polite & elegant form of speech, nor is it my purpose to do so at this time. For the Question itself demands exact proofs rather than rhetorical periods. Say then clearly, & without dissimulation what you think about the truth of this Question.

RESPONDENT. *The more briefly you speak, omitting circumlocutions, the more pleasing you will be to me, & clearer, and I promise you, & engage to observe most heedfully, to use the same brevity in answering, as you in propounding. I say therefore there is nothing in this question that I would not dare to defend most truthfully & certainly.*

QUEST. All is then well. I will anon cause danger to your forces, and I hope I shall so deal with you that it will soon appear to all how unequal you are to setting forth that which you have so rashly and boldly undertaken.

RESP. *You err, & do not know me, my good sir, if you think you can put me to flight with your harsh words. You have, as it happens, a spirited adversary, & one whom you will not conquer as easily as you think. Were you Hercules himself, or stouter than Polyphemus, or more boastful than Terentian Thraso, I neither stand in awe of your forces, nor shall make light of the bombast in your words.*

QUEST. Thus then I rise against the first question. There are many nouns which can be referred to no declension: therefore the first proposition is false.

112

DISPVTATIVN-
culaum Grammaticalium li-
bellus, ad puerorum in Scholis tri-
uialibus exacuenda ingenia primum excogita-
tus: iam vero denuo reuifus, & non pœnitenda obie-
ctionum & folutionum multitudine, ad magnum ftudio-
forum emolumentum & vtilitatem auctus, & cumu-
latus, opera & induftria IOANNIS STOC-
VVOODI, Scholæ Tunbridgienfis
olim Ludimagiftri.

QVÆ IN HAC EDITIONE
funt adiecta, quæftionum index, verfis
aliquot pagellis, facile com-
monftrabit.

SVNT AVTEM HIC OMNIA,
ad faciliorem explicationem & intelligen-
am eorum quæ in Regia Grammatica tra-
duntur & docentur, accom-
modata.

LONDINI,
Excudebat Th. Iudfon pro Ioanne
Harrifon iuniore, habitante in Pater nofter
rowe, fub figno aureæ Anchoræ,
1585.

TITLE-PAGE OF STOCKWOOD'S *DISPVTATIVNCVLARVM*
GRAMMATICALIVM LIBELLVS

This little book is entirely in Latin. The preface indicates that it was
published in 1598 (possibly a typographical error)

RESP. *The mountains labour, & a ridiculous little mouse is born* . . .

After these preliminary studies the boy was ready to begin his work on the Latin classics, some lists of which are given in the courses of study. According to Hoole the boy would begin this work at eight or nine years. The Lower School in Brinsley's list worked on Tully, Ovid, and Virgil, and at Harrow the three lower forms studied Cicero, Cato, Terence, and Ovid. H. R. D. Anders, in his *Shakespeare's Books*, cites references found in Shakespeare to Cæsar, Cicero, Ovid (with many instances where the poet obviously had in mind the original, and not Golding's translation), Virgil, Horace, Plautus, Seneca, Livy, Pliny, Lucan, and Juvenal. These references are found on pages 20–38 of Anders's book; they make interesting reading, and prove that Shakespeare knew these Roman authors, and knew them well.

NICHOLAS CLENARDUS wrote a Greek Grammar that analyzed the verbs and nouns and classified them. It was first published at Louvain in 1530. For a long time it was the one commonly used in France, and is in fact the principal basis of those lately or still in use among us, such as the Eton Greek Grammar. My copy was published by Aldus in 1570. It formerly belonged to the Duke of Sussex, with his bookplate.

Friar's School. Bangor, 1568.

Nothing shall be taught in said school but only grammar and such authors as concern the Latin and Greek tongues. [Clenardus's Greek Grammar is mentioned.]

1583. St. Bees Grammar School

The Greek Grammar of Clenard or some other generally allowed.

The "less Greek" of Ben Jonson, like the "little Latin," compared with our day, may have been a good deal.

At Harrow, in 1590, they had in the fourth form Grammatica Græca, and in the fifth form Demosthenes, Isocrates, Hesiod, Heliodorus, and Dionysius Halicarnasseus Græce.

IVLIO . GLORIERIO
ROMANO
ORDINIS . CISTERCIENSIS
EQVITI . NOBILISS.
ALDVS . MANVTIVS
PAVLLI . F . ALDI . N.
S. P. D.

C VM multa homines habeant, quae Deo Opt. Max. accepta quotidie referre debeant, nihil, si quis diligentius secum reputet, Ratione maius, nihil non dicam in homine, sed in omni caelo, ac terra praeclarius, nihil, quod propius ad Archetypum ipsum accedat, si uiris sapientibus credimus, haberi, excogitari ue potest. haec nos a brutis plane disiungit: haec alium alio praestantiorem reddit: haec omnia cernit, principia, caussasq. rerum uidet: haec quid faciendum, fugiendum ue sit, optime edocet,

✳ 2   atque

FIRST PAGE OF CLENARDUS'S GREEK GRAMMAR

RHETORIC

WILSON'S Rhetoric is the second book on the subject printed in the English language, Cox's being the first. Wilson emphasizes the importance of the order of words. In discussing faults of composition he says,

> Some will set the carte before the horse, as thus. My mother and my father are both at home, euen as thoughe the good man of the house ware no breaches, or that the graye Mare were the better Horse.

Wilson's general principles, which will be denied by none, are as follows:

> The ende of Rethorique.
> Three thynges are required of an Orator.
> To teache.
> To delight.
> And to perswade.

> First therefore an Orator muste labour to tell his tale, that the hearers maie well knowe what he meaneth, and vnderstande him wholy, the whiche he shall with ease do, if he vtter his mind in plain wordes, suche as are vsually receiued, and tell it orderly, without goyng aboute the busshe. That if he doe not this, he shall neuer do the other. For what manne can be delited or yet be perswaded, with the onely hearyng of those thynges, whiche he knoweth not what thei meane.

After describing the means of delighting his audience by a good voice and diction, he continues thus:

> Thirdly, suche quicknesse of witte must be shewed, and suche pleasaunt sawes so well applied, that the eares maie finde muche delite, whereof I will speake largely, when I

117

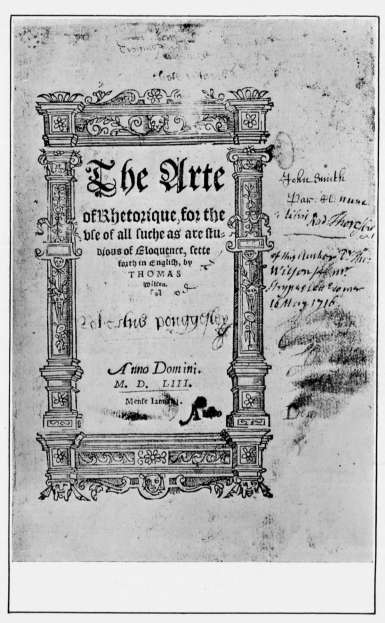

TITLE-PAGE OF WILSON'S *ARTE OF RHETORIQVE*

shall entreate of mouyng laughter. And assuredly nothyng is more nedefull, then to quicken these heauie loden wittes of ours, and muche to cherishe these our lompishe and unweldie natures, for excepte menne finde delight, thei will not long abide: delight theim, and wynne them: werie theim, and you lose theim for euer. And that is the reason, that menne commonly tary the ende of a merie plaie, and cannot abide the halfe hearyng of a sower checkyng Sermon. Therefore, euen these auncient preachers, must now and then plaie the fooles in the pulpite, to serue the tickle eares of their fleetyng audience, or els thei are like some tymes to preache to the bare walles . . . We shall get the good willes of our hearers, foure maner of waies, either beginnyng to speake of our selfes, or els of our aduersaries, or els of the people, and company present, or last of all, if we begin of the matter it self.

The letter of Don Armado in *Love's Labour's Lost* is said to be modeled on one of Wilson's examples; and Sir Walter Raleigh recently pointed out that there is a similarity between some of Falstaff's speeches and some of those offered as models in Wilson.

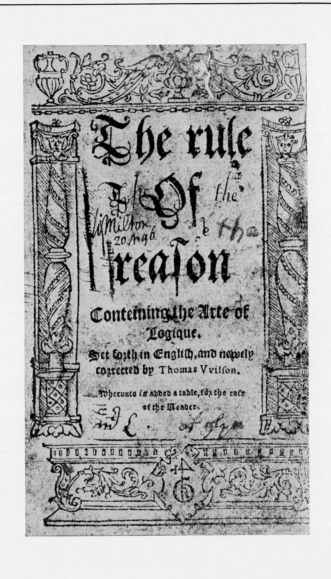

TITLE-PAGE OF WILSON'S *RULE OF REASON*

LOGIC

THE first edition of Wilson's *Rule of Reason* appeared in 1552, and another in 1567. My library has a copy of each. The book was dedicated to Edward VI. In the dedicatory Epistle of the first edition the author says:

> I knowe, your grace for your owne study litle nedeth any helpe of suche an Englyshe treatise, beyng so wel traueiled both in the Greke, & in the Latin for the same purpose, throughe the helpe of those right worthie men *Sir Ihon Cheke*, and *Sir Anthony Cooke*, your Maiesties teachers & Schole maistres in all good literature. But to fede and to satisfie the thirste and desire of suche Englishemen, as for defaulte of the said tongues could otherwise not come to the knowlege of *Logique*: I haue iudged it labour worth to geue ў preceptes & Rules therof in English . . .

A brief declaracion in metre, of the seuen liberall Artes,
wherein Logique is comprehended as one of them.

> Grāmer doth teache to vtter wordes
>   To speake bothe apt and plain.
> Logique by art, settes furthe the truthe,
>   And doth tell what is vain.
> Rethorique at large paintes well the cause
>   And makes that seme right gaie,
> Vvhich Logique spake but at a worde,
>   And taught as by the waie.
> Musike with tunes, delightes the eare:
>   And makes vs thynke it heauen:
> Arithmetique by nomber can make
>   Reckenynges to be eauen.
> Geometry, thynges thicke and brode,
>   Measures by line and square:
> Astronomie by sterres doth tell:
>   Of foule and eke of faire.

The first sentence of the textbook proper contains a very sound piece of advice.

> In euery cause that manne doth handle, this one lesson should first be learned. Neuer to entre upon any matter, nor yet once to talke without good aduisement.

Wilson then discusses logic, and the difference between logic and rhetoric.

> Bothe these Artes are muche like, sauing that Logique is occupied aboute all matters, and doeth plainly and nakedly set furth with apt wordes, the some of thinges, by the waie of argumentacion. Again of thother side, Rethorique useth gaie painted sentences, & setteth furth those matters with freshe colours and goodly ornamentes, and that at large. In so muche that zeno beyng asked the difference, betwene Logique and Rethorique, made answere by demonstracion of his hande, declaryng that when his hand was closed, it resembled Logique, when it was open and stretched out, it was like Rethorique. . . .

THE OFFICE OF LOGIQUE

> . . . There bee foure partes of this office or duetie, whereunto Logique is bounde. That is: To define the nature of euery thyng, to diuide, to knit true argumentes, and unknit false.

Taking up the discussion of the duty of making a definition, Wilson says that we must notice five kinds of words which mark the genus, species, differentia, proprium and accidens of the thing defined. As —

> Genus "a liuyng creature"
> Species "man"
> Differentia "endued wtih reason"

122

Proprium "able to speake." "whosoeuer hath power gevē him of nature to speake, that same body is a mā ... whosoeuer hath power to barke, that same is a dogge."
Accidens "mirth, sorwe" etc.

After definition comes division, and so on through an exhaustive discussion of the whole subject.

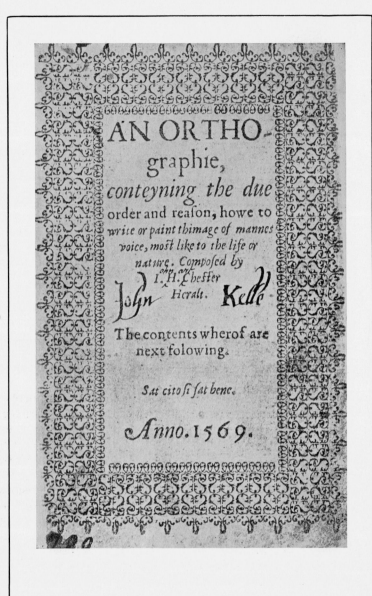

TITLE-PAGE OF JOHN HART'S *ORTHOGRAPHIE*

ORTHOGRAPHY

JOHN HART'S *Orthographie* was printed in 1569. The author introduces some reforms, and says that a number of people will object to his book:

> But in the moderne & present maner of writing (aswell of certaine other languages as of our English) there is such confusion and disorder, as it may be accounted rather a kinde of ciphring, or such a darke kinde of writing, as the best and readiest wit that euer hath bene, could, or that is or shalbe, can or may, by the only gift of reason, attaine to the ready and perfite reading thereof, without a long and tedious labour, for that it is vnfit and wrong shapen for the proportion of the voice. Whereas the new maner hereafter (thoughe it seeme at the first very straunge, hard and unprofitable) by the reading only thereof, will proue it selfe fit, easie and delectable, and that for whatsoeuer English may be writtē in that order.
>
> Yet I knowe that some at the first opening of the booke, and seeing of the straunge figures and maner of writing, wil say, what shal we now be set to schoole againe euen to our A.B.C.? then had we liued to long. Here are faire promises, like to this, that the toppes of trees shalbe planted in the grounde, and the rootes spred in the aire, and beare so their fruits, with such other rashe derisions as doe make me laugh when I thinke on them. And so considering the common opinion of mankinde to be so earnestlye giuen to thimitation of their predecessors condicions and maner of doings, and (as it were with tooth and nayle) to maintaine for the best, those wherein they themselues haue bene trayned and vsed from their Cradell, I haue stayed from publishing hereof many yeares.

John Hart's reforms produce a simplified spelling of which an example may be interesting.

Hart uses, among other new symbols, a script *d* for *th*, a figure resembling our numeral 8 for *sh*, and Ϭ for *ch*.

> / an experiens hou-an / ingli8man mẹ pronouns *d*e / fren8 bei *d*'order observd in *d*is niu maner, *d*oh hi-understand not *d*e / fren8, muϬ nerer *d*ẹr kómon spiϬ, *d*en bei *d*er oun maner ov wreiting.

" The Table of the Contentes" shows the book's scope:

> The Preface, wherein is brieflye conteyned the reasons, causes, commodities, summe and effect of this treatise.
> What letters are, and of their right use. Cap. j.
> How some men maintaine our abused English writing. Cap. ij.
> Of the diverse vices which use maintaineth in our writing, and howe they are particularly by reason confuted. Cap. iij.
> Of the number of our vowels, and of their auncient sounds in which they are alwayes used in the newe maner hereafter, by which their perfite use, our present abused sond of some of them, are found to be Dipthongs. Cap. iiij.
> The number of our Consonants and breaths, which we use in our speach, with the leaving of superfluous letters, and receyving of such others as we nede, — & examples of their right use. Cap. v.
> Of the accidentes of voweles, to weete, time, tune and breath with examples of Diphthongs and Triphthongs, with an order of distinction and pointing used thereafter. Cap. vj.
> An exercise (in the newe manner of writing) of that which is sayd, wherein is declared howe the rest of the Consonantes are made by the instruments of the mouth, which was omitted in the premisses, so that wee did not much abuse them. Cap. vij.
> Examples how certain other nations do sound their letters both in Latine and in their mother tongue, thereby to know the better how to pronounce their speaches, and so to reade them as they doe. Cap. viij.
> And a table at the ende, whereby the reader of the new maner may easilye finde the especiall and perticuler matters conteyned in this booke.

DICTIONARIES

IN THE Statutes of the Coventry Grammar School, not far from Stratford, dictionaries were, in 1628, ordered to be chained in their places.

The first English Dictionary, *Promptorium Parvulorum* (1440), by Galfridus Grammaticus, a Dominican monk, was printed by Pynson.

Bangor Friar School Statutes

Item. Besides the said Ordinary lectures the schoolmaster or Husher by the schoolmaster's appointment shall every night teach their scholars their Latin words with the English signification which their Latin words with their English significations every one of the scholars shall render without the books openly in the midst of the school so that the schoolmaster may hear and inform them every morning at their first coming to the school.

Item. They shall begin with words that concern the head reciting orderly as nigh as they can every part and number of the body and every particular of the same, after that they shall teach the names of sickness, diseases, virtues, vices, fishes, fowls, birds, beasts, herbs, shrubs, trees, and so forth they shall proceed in good order to such things as may be most frequented and daily used.

Foster Watson

Sir Thomas Elyot's Dictionary

Elyot's Latin-English Dictionary was the first published in England (1538). It fulfilled the purposes of a dictionary of biography and mythology as well as of a wordbook. I quote a half-column at random:

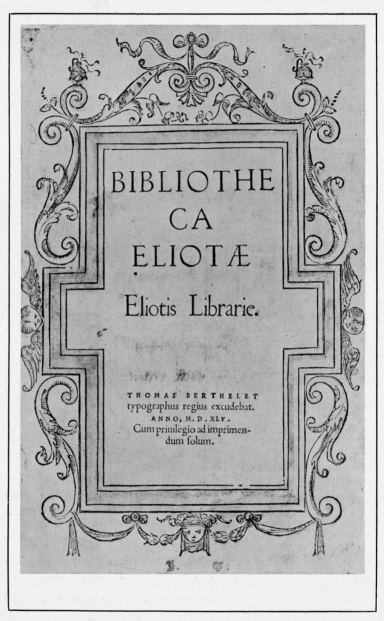

BIBLIOTHE
CA
ELIOTÆ

Eliotis Librarie.

THOMAS BERTHELET
typographus regius excudebat.
ANNO, M.D.XLV.
Cum priuilegio ad imprimen-
dum folum.

TITLE-PAGE OF ELYOT'S DICTIONARY, *BIBLIOTHECA
ELIOTÆ*

Ariadne, a lady, the wyfe of Theseus, whom he forsoke, not withstanding that she had saued his lyfe.

Aricia, a citie in Italy.

Aricinum nœmus, a woode by the sayde citie, where Numa kynge of Romaynes fayned to speake with Aegeria, the fairy.

Aricinus lacus, a brooke by Aricia.

Ariditas, dryenesse.

Aridus, drye.

Arida uita, a straight lyfe.

Aridus uictus, harde fare.

Aridus homo, a drye felowe, of whom nothyng may be gotten. som do call hym a pelt, or a pynchebeke.

Aries, etis, a ram. Also a piece of ordynaunce or ingine, made lyke a rammes head, to beat downe a wall. It is alsoo one of the. xii. signes that the sun passeth by. It is al o a fyshe hauynge hornes lyke to a ramme, whyche he some-tyme holdeth with his heade out of the water, and if he espye any man swymmynge, he goethe vnto hym, and pulleth hym vnder the water, and deuoureth hym.

Arietinus, of a ramme.

Arieto, aui, are, to hytte or throwe downe.

Arimaspi, people in Scithia, whiche haue but one eie, and that is in theyr foreheade, whyche do fyght contynually with gryphons or grypes. Herodotus sayth, that they haue. ii. eyes, but they vse to winke with the one, that they may haue the other more stedfast whan they do shote.

Whithals' Dictionary, about 1554, *a littell dictionarie for children*, is arranged according to subjects, so that "Whatere a child wants he can find it both in English and Latin with phrases in connection with words vsed." The object of the dictionary was to enable the child to acquire Latin for speaking as well as for writing, and the book had an extensive circulation. When purchased, my copy was supposed to be the only one in existence, but others have since been discovered.

Halec, is vsed for an hearyng.
Halecula, a pilcherde.
A scull of fishe, examen, nis.
A mermayden, syren nis.
A nitre, remora, echeneis.
grece.
Alga, wedor reites of the sea.

Shell fysshe.

A lopster, locusto, vel astacus,
ci, carabus, bi.
A crabbe, cancer, cri.
A tortes or shell padde, testu-
do, dinis. Sed testudo inter-
dum alia significat.
Cheloniū, the shel of a tortes.
A shrympe, squilla, nomen ge
nerale est.
A welk, turbo, nis, strōb⁹ gre
ce, coclea marina. Aliquando
coclea sumitur pro testa.
A cuckle, cōcha, che, (limacis.
An oyster, ostreum, trei, & o-
strea, treæ.
The oyster shell, testa, tæ: vel
testula, læ.
A muscle, mitulus, li.
Pisces saxatiles dicuntur, qui
in petris stabulentur.

Fresshe water fisshe.
Pisces fluuiatiles.

¶ Fresshe water fisshe, piscis
fluuiatilis.

A luce, lucius, crj.
A pyke, lupus fluuiatilis.
A troute fishe, varius.
A carpe, carpio, onis.
A cheuen, laccia.
A barbell, barbos, bi, vel tra-
gopogus.
A tenche, orphus lacustris.
Item tincha vocatur.
A perch, percala, l'percis, cidis
A lamprey, murena, fluta, vel
lampetra.
A creuis, gammarus, ri.
A prane, carides,
An pele, anguilla, læ.
Anguillariū, locus vbi abun-
dant anguillæ.
A leache called a horsleache or
blud sucker, hirudo, dinis, san
guisuga.
A frogge, rana, næ.
Coaxat rana.
The tadpoles of frogges or
toades, blowen in marche, cy-
rini dicuntur.

A ship with other
water vessels. &c.

Nauis cum pertinencijs. &c.
¶ A ship, nauis, uis.
He that maketh the ship, naui
pegus, gi.
The keele or bottom of a ship,
carina, næ.

Ays

The title-page (missing from my copy) is as follows:

> A Dictionary in English and Latine; devised for the capacitie of Children and young Beginners. At first set forth by M. Whithals, with Phrases both Rythmicall and Proverbiall: Recognized by Dr. Evans; after by Aber. Fleming and then by William Clerk.

"To avoid all Barbarisms and Anglicisms" Whithals' Dictionary was recommended.

The title-page of John Higgins's revision of Richard Huloet's *Dictionarie* reads, in part, as follows:

> Huloets Dictionarie, newelye corrected, amended, set in order and enlarged, vvith many names of Men, Tovvnes, Beastes, Foules, Fishes, Trees, Shrubbes, Herbes, Fruites, Places, Instrumentes &c. And in eche place fit Phrases, gathered out of the best Latin Authors. Also the Frenche thereunto annexed, by vvhich you may finde the Latin or Frenche, of anye Englishe woorde you will. By Iohn Higgins late student in Oxeforde.

The original publication was in 1552. It is described as an abecedarium for schoolboys. There were only two issues, although Higgins left a copy prepared for an enlarged reprint. Stevens quotes frequently from it in his notes on Shakespeare's plays. The British Museum copy of this edition (1572) lacks four leaves; mine is complete.

Example

(The page is headed " L. ante A".)

Laughe, Edere risus. Rideo, es. *Rire,. S.* Risum captare vel concitare. Ang. To cause men to laugh, *Faire rire les gens,. S.*

Laughe farre of. Prorideo es. *

Laughe immoderatlp. Cachinno, as. Et Cachinnor, naris. *Rire fort & desmesureement. S.*

Laughe hartelp. Perrideo es. *

131

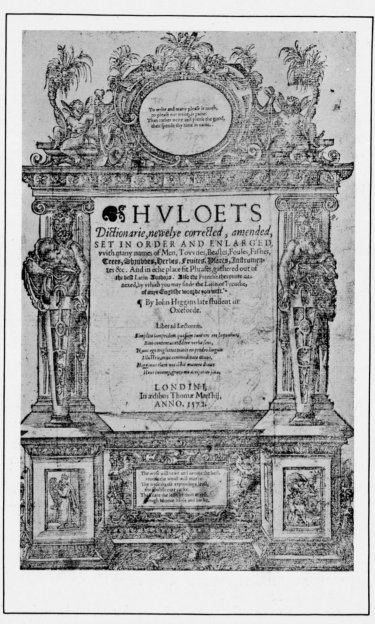

TITLE-PAGE OF HIGGINS'S REVISION OF
HULOET'S *DICTIONARIE*

Laughe mockingly, to mocke, derxde, floute, or jeste at, or to laugh to scorne.
Cachinnor, aris, Derideo, es. Obrideo, es. Irrideo, es. Pro
ridiculo habere, vel putare, Subsanno, as. *Se mocquer,
mocquer.*
Laughe priuely. Subrideo, es. *se subrire, S.*
Laughe, whereby to cause other to laughe.
Perrisio, sere, *.

Higgins says in the preface,

> At first I toke this worke of Maister Huloets in hande
> (gentle Reader) onelye to enlarge, and when I had herein
> passed some painefull time, I perceyued it almost a more
> easye matter to make new, then to amende : for there were
> many such woordes, as eyther serued not for the matter, or
> were out of use. Yet sith I had taken so much paynes
> therein, and brought therto welnighe then a Thousand
> words and Phrases, I thought not so to lease my labour &
> forsake the enterprise, but once againe toke penne in hande,
> and such woordes as were not sufficient (by consent of
> authorytie) I eyther displaced, and put farre bettter in
> their roumes, or if they were doubtfull, confirmed by
> sclender authority, or els serued the place but not so fitlye,
> I gaue them an Asteriske . . .

An *Alvearie or Quadruple Dictionarie* in "English, Latine,
Greeke, and French" by John Baret, Fellow of Trinity
College, Cambridge, 1573 (later edition, 1580), is dedicated to Lord Burghley. Apparently it was so popular that
scholars sang a chorus of praise, for it has nine prefatory
poems in Latin (one of them by Mulcaster) and three in
English. They are in flowery phrases :

> And Barret here (good Reader) doth present
> A Hyue of honie to thy gentle hand,
> By tract of time in painefull labor spent :
> Well wrought, and brought to such perfection and
> Good purpose, as (if truth be rightly scand)
> Thou art to blame, but if thou be his detter
> Of earned thankes, and fare by him the better.

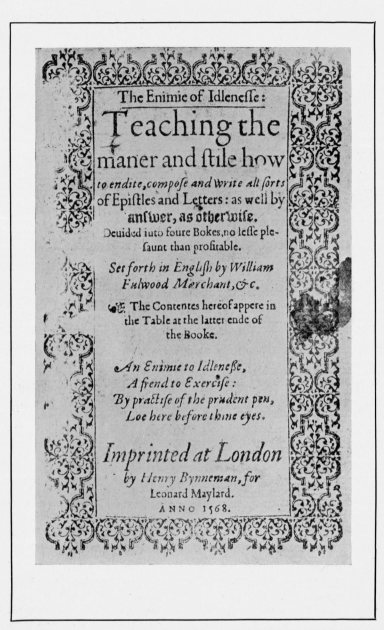

The Enimie of Idlenesse:

Teaching the maner and ſtile how to endite, compoſe and write all ſorts of Epiſtles and Letters: as well by anſwer, as otherwiſe. Deuided iuto foure Bokes, no leſſe pleſaunt than profitable.

Set forth in Engliſh by William Fulwood Merchant, &c.

The Contentes hereof appere in the Table at the latter ende of the Booke.

An Enimie to Idleneße,
A frend to Exerciſe:
By practiſe of the prudent pen,
Loe here before thine eyes.

Imprinted at London *by Henry Bynneman, for* Leonard Maylard. ANNO 1568.

TITLE-PAGE OF FULWOOD'S *ENIMIE OF IDLENESSE*

LETTER WRITING

THE Rivington Grammar School Statutes of 1566, quoted in Foster Watson's *English Grammar Schools to 1660*, say:

> And the elder sort must be exercised in devising and writing sundry epistles to sundry persons of sundry matters, as of chiding, exhorting, comforting, counselling, praying, lamenting, some to friends, some to foes, some to strangers; of weighty matters, or merry, as shooting, hunting, &c., of adversity, or prosperity, of war, and peace, divine and profane, of all sciences, and occupations, some long and some short; or else in making verses, orations and declamations, and noting the parts of them . . . according to the rules of rhetoric.

I give two letters from the choice collection in William Fulwood's *Enimie of Idlenesse: Teaching the maner and stile how to endite, compose and write all sorts of Epistles and Letters*, the first edition of which appeared in 1568.

A LOUER REQUESTETH HIS LADIES LOUE.

Considering (my soueraigne ioy) the great vertues of nobilitie, beautie, and curtesie, wherewith nature by superabundant measure hath in such sort decored you, that aboue all other terrestriall bodies you are iudged by common voice to obtaine the Crowne and principalitie: And on the other side waying the want and insufficiencie of my former seruices towards you, my trembling hande is scarce able to holde the penne, neither dare my stammeryng tongue expresse that which the afflicted heart through ardent appetite desireth to manifest vnto you. Yet Loue (which aboue all animated creatures, holdeth in his domination my inflamed mynd) doth so exceede, that it giueth me doutful boldnesse, to take in hande to open vnto you the secrets of my brest: which is to doe you to vnderstand, ý euer since mine eyes did speculate & beholde your great beautie, my hart hath remained so bound & intangled, ý of it owne free wil it hath chosen to bee included in youre swete prison. By reason wherof, & seing the vexations and greuous passions of my languishing corpse, caused through the swete regard of your eyes, & augmēted by ý great eclipsatiō of your absence, I am constrained to implore and demaūde your aide and succor. And bicause you are she, who only & none other, may sēd remedie in this case, I therefore moste humbly pray and request you, that euē as in all other vertues you ar souerain, so likewise in this matter you woulde shew your selfe charitable and pitifull. And sith you are y̆ cause of this so great and greuous martirdome, and that you only may help and remedie it, extende therefore the true remedie, by sendyng a benigne aunswere, the which I moste effectuously desire and attende.

THE AUNSWER OF HIS LADY

My trobled thought so discordeth frō your fonde affection, that I cannot maruell inough to imagine what cause moued you, & gaue you such presūptuous boldnesse, as to trouble & interrupt me of mine accustomed reste, throughe your abhominable letters and wanton wordes. Your saide letters (to the ende that they shoulde not come vnto the handes of any other person) I haue receiued: and beholding the contentes therof, with great paine could I bridle mine ire, and withholde my selfe from tearing them in peeces: but considering that such fault is not to be imputed vnto the letters which are insensible, but vnto the composer and doer of them, I therefore refrayned my selfe from that purpose, willing to exercise that myne anger and rigor vpon the messanger: but likewise for reporte sake, I refrayned, gyuyng hym speciall charge, not thenceforth to returne vnto me with any such message. And to the ende that you shall not presume to continue any longer in this sute, vnderstande ye that I am not she, vnto whome such abusiue letters should be sente. I haue thought good (contrary to myne accustomed maner) to write vnto you at this present, which my spirite wyth much adoe can scarce abide to finish, through the great offence that it feeleth : certifying you, that if you perseuer any longer in this matter, you shall doe vnto me a moste displeasant thing, and vnto youre selfe shall purchase great & euident damage. Wherefore I praye you (for the auoyding of all these inconueniences) that you wil condescende vnto my request : and so doinge you shall doe me a singular pleasure.

I have now finished a short survey of such of the books for teachers, the courses of study of Shakespeare's time, and the textbooks likely to have been used at Stratford as are in my library.

The pedagogical books, the course of study, the textbooks, the instruction by three university graduates, give one a splendid idea of what the Stratford Grammar School was like at the time Shakespeare entered it. The basis of instruction was Latin, for that language was the key to all knowledge. During those years no time was spent on modern history, geography, French or German, or "nature study"; the child went a long way in the Latin language and literature, so that a boy's knowledge of the classics was better than that of the average college graduate in America now.

This was the same sort of education as that given to Chaucer, Spenser, Bacon, and even Milton, in their schooldays. The plays of Shakespeare are full of classical allusions, all of which might refer to what he learned in the school in Stratford and in his subsequent readings of his contemporaries. It seems to me that Shakespeare's brief schooling must have resulted in considerably more learning than the layman has credited him with.

His education, however, cannot account for his success. It contributed something, it was a solid foundation, a preparation for further study; but although others, indeed very many, had the same opportunities, yet we have only one Shakespeare.

Date Due